The Way to Write Novels

By the same author

Novels:
Lying-in
A Fleshly School
Linsey-Woolsey
Paradise
The Marriage Ring (with Dulan Barker)
A Pillar of Cloud
The Golden Veil
Barnwell

Biography:
Gerard Manley Hopkins
A Most Unsettling Person: Patrick Geddes (1854-1932)

Travel:
Poets' London

SERIES EDITORS JOHN FAIRFAX & JOHN MOAT

The Way to Write Novels

PADDY KITCHEN

June B. P. MacCunn
12 August 1989
Leeds

Elm Tree Books • London

First published in Great Britain 1981
by Elm Tree Books Ltd/Hamish Hamilton Ltd
27 Wrights Lane London W8 5TZ
Reprinted 1986

British Library Cataloguing in Publication Data

Kitchen, Paddy
The way to write novels.
1. Fiction — Authorship
I. Title
808.3'3 PN3365

ISBN 0-241-10648-6
ISBN 0-241-10649-4 Pbk

Filmset by Pioneer
Printed and Bound in Great Britain by
Redwood Burn Ltd, Trowbridge

Contents

Chapter One

Intention

Your Intention

It would be impertinent of me to assert why I think you may have begun to read this book. The variations of motive that prompt writers and would-be writers to find out more about their potential are incalculable. But I will try to plot a range of experience within which you may find an equivalence.

You may already have completed one, or more, novel-length manuscripts. Perhaps you have submitted them to publishers without success. Perhaps you are diffident about showing your work. But you are still interested in those piled-up pages — they are unfinished business.

Some of you may have begun novels, and then faltered. You may wonder how to go on, or whether it is really worth going on.

There may be those who cherish the idea of writing a novel, but are too modest or unconfident to begin. Usually such people are diffident because they are discriminating and admiring readers.

And some may have had experience in completing, and perhaps publishing, short pieces, but are daunted by the idea of setting out on a journey of some 60,000 words.

A few of you may have a theme, a life-experience, that seems to need a novel for its expression, but don't know where to begin.

And perhaps some of you enjoy writing, would like to earn some money, and wonder whether it is worth just having a bash — at weekends, after the children are in bed, between jobs, or during the holidays.

What I assume we all have in common, however, is an interest in the idea of writing a novel. By which I do not mean an interest in achieving literary fame or a particular life-style, but an interest in the novel itself. Should you find novel-reading rather a bore, and the things you write pretty dull, then no amount of ambition to become a novelist because it sounds glamorous will do. *Interest* —

shining, intense, exuberant, painful, painstaking, passionate interest in the existence and creation of prose fiction is essential.

'I think everyone who does not *need* to be a writer, who thinks he can do something else, ought to do something else,' said Simenon in an interview. He added that he considered writing to be 'not a profession, but a vocation of unhappiness.' I don't share that extreme view, but I would never recommend it as a comfortable occupation.

The two things most often said about being a writer are that it is hard work and that it is lonely — bald statements that by themselves do not mean very much. It can be hard work, but so can nursing, mining or deep-sea diving. And it is lonely in the sense that you work by yourself, but it is that very condition that so often appeals to people. To have an occupation that requires only a quiet space, paper, and a writing instrument — what heaven! As someone who likes to work on my own, I agree. But working entirely on one's own can be difficult for two reasons.

The first concerns discipline. While writing can be a fluent, joyous process, it can also be the difficult chore you want to avoid at all costs. However, like singing, swimming, dieting or meditating you have to keep at it regularly if you're to achieve anything. The second reason is the lack of feedback. Most jobs and occupations bring contact with other people. That contact is not always pleasant, yet the actual process of commands, consultations, assessments, disagreements, achievements, failures — mostly on a very minor scale — carry one through the working day and give it automatically a content and a tempo. But whether your writing day consists of sitting gloomily in front of a blank piece of paper or enthusiastically finishing two whole chapters, there will be no outside feedback; just the blank page to greet you the following morning, or a pile of manuscript to read and correct.

Which is not to say that the intending novelist must have iron self-discipline and unshakable self-sufficiency; that could mean a lack of sensitivity or imagination. But anyone who is chronically disorganised and normally needs constant company does start with a handicap.

My intention

I will not be able to tell you *how* to write your novel, and certainly not how to sell it. But I will try to illuminate and share aspects of the process of writing, and I will describe some of the practicalities that surround the business of being published.

I have no set of rules which, if followed faithfully, will lead to success.

And, incidentally, what did *you* think I meant by that word 'success'? A tax exile's mansion? A single published volume? Or a laudatory review in the *Times Literary Supplement*?

I must bear in mind that you might privately want to emulate any novelist from Jackie Collins to William Golding; bear in mind too Henry James's remark that the novel 'will stretch anywhere – it will take in absolutely anything'. And I must remember also that perhaps you do not want to emulate anybody, but to produce work that seems as innovatory and exciting as *Ulysses* did sixty years ago.

Incidentally some of you may wonder whether to believe those who say that writing can't be taught. Obviously it can't be taught like French or mathematics – progressively more difficult dollops of information handed out for inhalation at regular intervals. But if teaching is in this case regarded as a dialogue, an exchange of perceptions, which involve a tutor willing to adapt to differing students, and students willing to listen to criticism and think hard about their work, then creative writing can be a heady subject both to teach and to learn. After all, most professional painters have been to art school.

Chapter Two

Beginnings

To decide to write a novel is a curious business. Unlike swimming the Channel, you do not need to tell anybody, to elicit aid. Not in the beginning.

But if it is ever to get further than just a beginning, a brief scurry into prose, the idea that sparks the novel has got to set in your consciousness with the potentiality and privacy of a seed in good soil.

The best time to embark on the writing is when the idea has been lodged in your mind for some time but you still show no signs of losing interest in it. To begin a novel when you are already slightly bored with the idea is futile. It needs to be running alive — nagging, unfolding.

You may already have notes or diaries or short pieces that connect with a theme. Get them all together and take a dispassionate look at them. Do they seem to add up to something, point towards further development? Do they still interest you? If so, perhaps try writing some more, filling in the gaps. Or re-writing what you already have: expanding it, drawing it together.

If you have not yet written anything that connects with your theme, sit down and do so. You don't necessarily have to begin at the beginning. Choose a key scene, or a particular emotional experience that is part of the complex that clusters around the theme, and write it out. Write as strongly, as feelingly, as you can. Don't be afraid. No one need see it. Then come back the next day and see what you've got. Perhaps continue that process for a week or two. Try to write something every day; that way it will become part of your life. As Hemingway said, 'You can write any time people will leave you alone and not interrupt you. Or rather you can if you will be ruthless enough about it.'

Now, having stepped on to the edge of a territory which may or may not turn into a novel, where do we go from here?

Briefly into the real world, the place where you live.

This is not true for everybody, but on the whole I think we all need a *place* to write. It is of course possible to write away from base — in the office, at the back of the classroom, on the beach — but it is helpful to have a base to come back to. It may be a dressing-table, one end of a sofa, a kitchen table, a bunk-bed in a shared room, or for the lucky a desk, but it is the place you claim for your writing. You may not tell anyone about it, but you claim it in your mind and return to it frequently, probably when you can be alone.

Privacy and space can present a problem. I personally believe that a writer *must* have both a place to write and a space to keep his 'things'. Indeed, I think you don't have to be a writer to need these facilities. Ideally everyone from the age of about ten should have a desk with drawers (lockable if preferred) or its equivalent. How else do you deal comfortably with letters, diaries, study, reading, and generally fiddling around with your thoughts?

What you keep in your space is an entirely personal matter. My own list of essentials would include: a good dictionary, *Roget's Thesaurus,* rough paper, A4 typing paper, carbon paper, envelopes, stamps, typewriter and several Edding 2100 pens in different colours.

The question of whether you do or don't work straight on to the typewriter is again entirely your decision. Some writers find word processors timesaving, others say they are a distraction. One thing is sure, they don't write the book for you.

Is it essential to type? No, if you can afford others to do it for you and have clear handwriting which they can read. But it makes life much, much simpler if you do. Even if you have final manuscripts typed professionally, it helps to distance you from your work at the early stages to see it in type. And you can at some point make a carbon which prevents that nerve-racking business of leaving one's only copy of a 400-page masterpiece on top of a bus on the way to the typist.

Having made a bid for space in the real world — back to the novel. Writing in the eighteenth century, Edward Young declared that original composition 'opens a back-door out of the bustle of this busy, and idle world, into a delicious garden of moral and intellectual fruits and flowers . . .', while Richard Ellmann in our own century has written, 'What seems to set off the creative process is a deflowering, a brutalisation of the soul by experience, experience which in some sense must be wished for.' Both statements are true for both centuries. It is very seldom that a good novel does not contain passages emanating from both states of mind — and many in between.

This is all very well, you may say, but what should my novel be *about*? I mean I have this experience at the back of my mind of when I was a refugee in Wales during the war and it links to my parents going to the seaside to retire — I can't really explain why —

but is that likely to turn into a novel?

And I can't answer that one. All I can say is — go to your writing space every day and get something down. Does the actual production of words, the immersion in your idea, make the theme more firm? Does it take hold? Does it, like a skeleton under flesh, seem to have a form to hold it together?

Or does it all just leak away, like a puddle in the lawn after a storm, and leave you with nothing you feel you can really work on? (Warning: don't answer that question two minutes, or even two days, after writing something; look at it two weeks, or preferably two months, later.)

To some this will all seem far too vague. You know the story you want to write, be it based on your experience as a social worker or a fantasy set in Atlantis, and you don't want to begin in the vague, unplanned way I have just described. You will begin at the beginning. But how far should you map your journey?

If you are going to have a complex plot, and particularly if your narrative is going to depend heavily on the development and pace of specific events, then it is essential to plan out the story. There is nothing more maddening than writing 150 pages only to discover that the confrontation you had intended around the end of Chapter 4 can't happen because one of the protagonists was unexpectedly imprisoned in Chapter 3. Obviously any story which relies on suspense and surprise must be carefully thought out. This doesn't mean that things can't be changed during the writing, but you do need to be assured from the start that your intended story actually contains the right ingredients to produce shocks and reversals.

And are you confident of depicting the scenes which you plan? You don't need to be run over to write about an accident, but can you describe it convincingly? It is possible to set a book in a continent you have never visited — Saul Bellow did it in his African novel *Henderson the Rain King* — but that continent needs to have quite a hold on your imagination. It is no good thinking your spies will go to Berlin just because John Le Carré's spies go there. Can you *see* Berlin in your mind? Your Berlin, I mean, not Le Carré's.

Above all, of course, are you going to sustain an interest in your characters for a whole book, and do you know enough about them to understand how the action will affect and change them? Some writers go so far as to have a card index with details of their characters' background, behaviour and appearance neatly recorded, though others would find this a cumbersome apparatus.

Don't stultify yourself with planning, but don't embark on Chapter 1 with just a whim and an anecdote.

Iris Murdoch finds planning the most important part. 'I invent the whole thing in enormous detail before I start writing at all. That can take longer than writing.' Others sail rather blindly into the first fifty pages or so and then stop and take stock. Is it going to work, is it worth pressing on? If the answer seems to be yes, then this is perhaps the stage to work out details of the rest of the plot. If the answer is no, well — put the pages away in a drawer. In a couple of years you might suddenly see how the idea could be developed after all.

Don't plead ignorance as a reason for not jumping in at the deep end. Some people pretend that they can't begin their novel until they've found out from the pros how many chapters it should have, or whether incest is an acceptable theme, or whether it should be typed on A4 or quarto, bank or bond. That is just prevarication. There is no point in believing you can only write a novel after you have gained access to a set of rules. Those rules don't exist. Stop looking over your shoulder and simply begin.

Chapter Three

For Those of You who Want to Reach the End as Soon as Possible

Some people need to prove to themselves that they can actually finish a full-length novel before they can begin to think of examining their work critically. I have much sympathy with them and this chapter is about the process of pulling oneself willy-nilly from page one to the end for the first time.

'I couldn't write a book,' a student will say. 'How do you ever finish so many pages?' My stock reply is, 'If you write one page a day for a year, you'll have quite a long novel.' And that would be one method of getting to the end.

Françoise Sagan's main problem when she started *Bonjour Tristesse* at the age of eighteen was whether she would be able to finish it. 'I wasn't thinking about "literature" and literary problems, but about myself and whether I had the necessary will-power.' In the end she completed it in three months, working two or three hours a day.

I wrote my first published novel during a month's holiday in a rented cottage with my mother and six-month-old son. I did fourteen pages every morning while my mother looked after Dan, and managed to complete the first draft in three weeks. I could not write that quickly, that freely, now. In those days I found it almost impossible to criticise something I had just written. Now I find it almost impossible to leave one sentence alone and go on to the next.

The first writer friend I had, Ann Quin, who published four highly original novels before her early death in 1973, remembered in an interview how hard she used to work when she first came to London in the fifties. 'I was working in a job from nine until six and going back to my room every evening, writing my first novel. I was about twenty, twenty-one and going back every evening and sitting down and conscientiously writing page after page every evening from seven until about midnight and I did this for about eighteen months.' That novel was never published, and nor was her next — an apprenticeship much more common than Françoise Sagan's immediate, youthful success.

If you choose a work rhythm, be it a page a day or twenty each weekend, an hour before breakfast or four hours after supper, try to stick to it. The only way to make the pile of pages grow is to write another page. Once you reach half way, the end becomes not only possible but probable. You've proved you can reach the middle of the tunnel so you might just as well press on to the light at the end.

How many words, how long? The tiresome but true answer is — whatever length seems right. 60,000 to 75,000 words is average. Anything under 50,000 is short — but that didn't stand in Sagan's way. And something like *The Far Pavilions* is about 500,000 words. This book is around 30,000.

There is one technical warning I will make here to those anxious to complete at all costs, and that is about the point of view or narrative voice. It is usual when students begin writing a story for them to adopt a narrative voice quite unconsciously.

It may be in the first person: 'I woke up and looked at John and for the first time during our marriage I had an urge to hit him, as he lay on his back, bald and somnolent and smelling of whisky.'

Or it may be in the third person, told mainly through the eyes of one character: 'Hélène woke up and looked at John and realised that for the first time during their marriage she would like to hit him. He lay there, bald and somnolent, smelling of whisky.'

Or it may be in the third person, with more than one viewpoint: 'Hélène woke up and looked at John and realised that for the first time during their marriage she would like to hit him. He lay there, dimly aware she was leaning over him, and knew that he smelled of whisky and that his bald head revolted her.'

Or it may be in the third person, but from an objective, general point of view: 'There were two heads on the pillows: one covered with soft, curling black hair, the other quite bald. The black-haired one moved, showing the pretty face of a young woman who yawned and propped herself on one elbow. As she leaned over the man, whose eyes were closed, she wrinkled her nose with what looked like disgust bordering on hate. A slight movement of the man's eyelids revealed that he was perhaps not quite asleep.'

These four openings reveal both some of the problems and the freedom which confront the novelist. It is possible to leap into a short story without thinking too much about the narrative voice, but it can lead to tangles and disappointments in the case of a novel.

If you adopt the first person, and it does have some advantages for the beginner, you restrict yourself from ever stating what any of the other characters are privately thinking, or from directly reporting action in which your main character is not involved. The advantage is that you need not be much more knowledgeable or sensitive about other characters' backgrounds or behaviour than your narrator is. I found this useful in my own first novel, since at that stage I could not go inside the heads of a varied cast of characters at all credibly.

With the third person, used mainly from one point of view, you avoid the trap of never being able to allow any but the central character to think (unless it be via speech), or to act separately. If, as in the first person narrative, one is mainly involved with, and anchored in, one character, it is necessary to bear lightly in mind that a switch to other characters needs to be done convincingly and not merely for convenience.

The narrative told from several points of view gives a wonderful freedom both in the exploration of emotional and psychological behaviour and in the development of a story. It is, however, more difficult to orchestrate: to balance the weight of each character and to pace the story. In my second novel I found I automatically switched to this type of plural viewpoint, but that there was a difference between my main characters and the minor ones. The four main people — two men and two women — came very much from inside my own head; I could quite easily assume their voices and their thoughts, although many of their characteristics were collected from outside observation. The minor characters, however, were altogether objective, 'heard' rather than 'spoken', 'seen' rather than 'felt'.

The fourth kind of narration I cited, the distanced, general view, is not often used continuously throughout a book but is intermingled with more personal narration, especially for descriptions of place and milieu, or as the equivalent of a film camera observing a total scene before it zooms in to focus on one particular character.

Again, it is clearly possible to have both first and third person narrative in the same novel, though this is quite difficult to bring off successfully.

In all these cases I am talking in terms of more-or-less conventional prose narrative. Those who are anxious to assimilate the complexities of unconventional writers over the ages, and to lay down their prose fictions in new forms and from original angles of the mind, will be pursuing singular paths and not wishing to tumble somewhat blindly through their first full-length manuscript.

'Blindly?' you might ask, in a critical tone. 'Surely one should write with awareness, not blindly?' Yes, on the whole; but here I am just trying to encourage those who want to finish in order to prove something to themselves. Sometimes it is necessary to hurl yourself at a difficult obstacle, forgetting all the techniques you were taught to enable you to clear easier ones elegantly. Henry Miller once said, 'You see, I think it's bad to think. A writer shouldn't think much.' Not an axiom for all time, but for some occasions.

And to my mind much worse than thinking is talking — talking about the novel you intend to write, that is. For it is perfectly possible to talk a novel into still-birth. Angus Wilson, in an interview, put his finger on the main reason: '. . . fiction writing is a kind of magic, and I don't care to talk about a novel I'm doing because if I communicate the magic spell, even in an abbreviated form, it loses its force for me.' This is true. As long as the idea matures and effervesces inside your head, it has life. But if you tell it to someone, and they are critical or indifferent, the idea easily loses some of its magic. And even if it is well-received, thereby encouraging you to tell more people, you are no longer so excited about committing it to paper. In my experience the only people to talk to about would-be novels are one or two other novelists who know me well and who are perfectly versed in the art of tentative reaction that just verges on encouragement.

But in the beginning, before meeting any published writers, the only way to find out whether my idea could be turned into a novel was to sit down and write it out.

Chapter Four

Some of the Practicalities of Publication

Strictly speaking, this chapter should be the penultimate one. We ought not to be talking about publishers and money until we have finished discussing writing and re-writing. But since publishers and money will be the topic some readers want to know about most, and as a number of those who have proved to themselves they can finish a novel may want to submit their efforts, it seemed sensible to tackle such practicalities now.

There is another reason too: I do not want to mislead anybody. I do not want anyone to think that provided they go through all the motions suggested in the following chapters they are bound to have a book published. They aren't, and one of the functions of this chapter is to explain why.

It has never been easy to get a first novel published, and in recent years it has become very difficult indeed. A publishing house is a business enterprise, and many are now part of large commercial conglomerates even though they still carry the well-known names and imprints of their founders. This means that if they accept a book for publication they need to be as sure as they can that it will not lose money, and their financial overlords would prefer them to be as sure as they can that it will make a substantial profit. During frequent meetings and discussions with sales, promotion and production staff, an editor may find it very difficult to defend the publication of a first novel which he personally likes, but which no one can anticipate will sell more than 500 copies — if that. And you would be surprised how many quite well-known authors sell no more than 1000 copies nowadays. The reasons are obvious: increase in the price of books, cutbacks in public library spending, many people no longer able to spare money to buy fiction in hardback.

That last reason usually prompts the question, 'Why aren't novels published straight away in paperback?' In fact some genre novels (science fiction, romance, western, etc.) are, but it would not surmount the problem for a conventional first novel. Paperback houses already publish too many titles for the bookshops to absorb all of them profitably, and in order to keep the price of a book down to a level acceptable to the public they would need to print far more copies than they could expect to sell of a first novel by an unknown author. Added to which there is the complication that not all bookshops devote shelf-space to paperbacks with limited appeal.

But some first novels become bestsellers, you may argue. To which I reply, 'Very, very, very (ad infinitum) few.' It's about as useless to hope that your first attempt (or indeed any attempt) at a novel will be a bestseller, as it is to imagine that should you be elected to your local council you will have a good chance of becoming Prime Minister. There are, remember, approximately 3,000 new novels published every year.

I do not believe that any of this is sufficient reason not to write a novel, but I think it should be taken realistically into account by anyone who is more interested in being published than they are in actually writing. Rejection slips can make people most dispirited. There might be better ways of employing valuable time.

Having said all that, however, I will just point to the obvious fact that publishers of fiction must take on some first novels or they won't have the steady-selling Lessings, Murdochs, Amises, Fowleses, Goldings and Highsmiths of the future for their lists.

The mechanics of submitting a manuscript are most adequately set out in *The Writers' & Artists' Yearbook* (published in paperback), which also gives the addresses of many British publishers, journals and literary agents, and much more besides. Briefly, a manuscript should be typed in double-spacing, most people use A4 paper, pages must be numbered, and a few corrections don't matter as long as the script is easily legible. Complicated binders are rather a nuisance — loose sheets in a cardboard wallet held by a stout rubber band will suffice. Do keep a carbon or photocopy, publishers have no legal responsibility for the safety of any manuscripts they receive.

When selecting a publisher, choose one that publishes books which fall more-or-less into the same category as yours. Do some research in your local library and bookshops, and keep an eye on the book reviews. You can also request publishers to send you their current catalogue.

You may prefer to write in the first instance to find out whether the publisher of your choice would like to consider your novel. Give a brief description of it, and if it is in a particular genre say so (more about genres in Chapter 8).

When submitting a manuscript always enclose the wherewithal to cover return postage, and a short letter explaining that you are sending your first novel, eg *The Unreadable Book*, for their consideration. If you have already received a letter prompting you to submit, mention it. Then sit back and wait.

It can be anything from a week to a year before your manuscript is returned, or the publishers contact you. It would be quite reasonable, if you have heard nothing for three months, for you to contact them, by letter, and enquire politely after your manuscript.

'How can I be certain they will read my novel?' Well obviously you can't, but provided the publishers you have selected are seeking new work I can assure you they will look at it, though they may not read it all the way through. 'That's not fair!' Yes, it is perfectly fair; if the first chapter is incompetent, boring, or too close to the plot of *Rebecca,* there is no reason why the publisher should read on — particularly if a glance at the last chapter reveals that it is still incompetent, boring, or too close to the plot of *Rebecca.*

As I hope the third paragraph of this chapter makes clear, it would be quite possible for a publisher's editor to like your novel but still to reject it. (In the present economic climate, quite a few established authors are having good novels turned down.) When that happens, or when they feel there is some particular merit in the writing, they may include a letter of encouragement with the returned manuscript rather than just a flat rejection. If they do, take a little cheer from it, but don't enter into a long correspondence with the writer of the letter — unless, of course, an answer has been invited. One of the reasons why publishers very seldom pass critical comment on unsolicited manuscripts is because they simply could not cope with the flood of correspondence this can perpetrate. Remember that the opinion of publishers' editors are, like those of any other readers, subjective: they are not speaking for the whole of the literary establishment. It is possible for a book to be turned down by seventeen publishers and accepted by an eighteenth.

Some readers may feel that in this chapter I seem thus far to have been on the side of publishers rather than writers. This is not so, but I do know how unreasonable writers can be in their expectations and I wish to be candid. Now, however, I am going to talk about what happens once a manuscript is accepted, and I suspect that many publishers will feel I err in favour of the writer. Again, this is not so: it is just that I realise how thoughtless publishers' behaviour can appear to be to an author. Partly this is due to misplaced expectations on the author's part, but this time I believe that they are often by no means unreasonable expectations.

I am not going to discuss publishers' contracts and their consequences in detail, but sketch briefly what the acceptance of a first novel might entail.

If the publishers accept the novel outright, they will probably say so in a letter and also say what advance against royalties they are prepared to offer. ('Advance against royalties' means a sum of money paid to the author in advance of any sales of his book. 'Royalties' are the percentage due to the author from the retail price of each copy sold.) If the person who writes to you indicates they might be willing to accept the book after some more work has been done on it, then you should perhaps find out what advance they have in mind and whether you agree with the suggested modifications — bearing in mind that when you have made them, they still might not take the book on.

An advance can vary from as little as £100 to as much (for an international bestseller) as £1,000,000. There are no rules to govern what you should be offered. The Writers' Guild has a specimen minimum terms contract which it is pressing for all publishers to agree, but so far only a few have. *The Writers' & Artists' Yearbook* will explain to you the services offered by both the Writers' Guild and the Society of Authors; both organisations will give advice to their members on publishers' contracts — which are quite complex documents. If in doubt, do seek advice. You want to have a fair deal for any future sales of subsidiary rights such as paperback, USA, film, etc, all of which will be included in the contract.

There is a simple method of working out what would be a fair initial advance for your book, though your publishers may not appreciate your employing it. Ask them how many copies of the book they intend to print, and what they estimate the retail price will be. Then, given that your royalty (on a hardback) for the first 5,000 copies sold should be not less than 10%, you can see whether their offer is fair.

For example, supposing they intend to sell the book at £8.00, your royalty on each copy will be 80p. If they order 1500 copies to be printed, they will distribute roughly 200 of these for review and promotion, which means they are hoping to sell the remaining 1300 copies. Your share of that total sale would be £1040 (1300 x 80p). So if you have been offered an advance of only £200 you are well entitled to ask for more. But if you have been offered £750, you aren't doing too badly given they may not sell all the 1300 — and, of course, if they do you will receive the outstanding royalties in due course. If they offer the whole £1040 (very unlikely), and only sell 300 copies of the book, you will not have to pay anything back (unless you have signed a most unorthodox contract), but a metaphorical little red cloud will hang over your name within the company's memory. (If a book takes off and becomes really successful, they will of course reprint — something which, alas, does not happen very often.)

An advance is not payable all at once; the usual procedure is to receive half on signature of the contract after the book is accepted, and half on publication. Sometimes the time gap between receiving the cheque and the day you returned the signed contract, or publication day, can seem unnecessarily long and as company cash flows grow more sluggish so the gaps apparently lengthen.

'Oh dear,' you may say, 'I really cannot cope with all this. I'm interested in literature, not haggling over money. Wouldn't it be better if I had an agent?'

The problem with that question is, it is nearly as difficult to find a good agent who will handle a first novel as it is to find a firm to publish it. I do not on the whole feel it is really worth seeking an agent at this stage, unless perhaps you are privy to some advice and put into direct contact with a recommended one. (Or unless you have it on good opinion that you have written a likely commercial success.) Unfortunately there is no way to find out which are the best agents for your work since unlike publishers they cannot display their wares. Also there is the minor factor that publishers rather like discovering new writers by themselves.

However, if and when writing becomes a major part of your career, then I think an agent can be one of the most important people in your life. And once you have had something published, agents will obviously be more eager to represent you, and you will be in a better position to decide which particular one is likely to suit your needs. The Association of Authors' Agents at 10 Buckingham Street, London WC2, will send you a list of their members, and membership of the association ensures a commitment to a code of professional practice and behaviour.

Once the publishers are happy with your final script, someone in the firm will copy-edit it. This means they will adapt it in minor matters to the house style (eg whether speech is within single or double inverted commas, whether words like 'recognise' are spelled with an 's' or a 'z') and correct any spelling or slight grammatical or style errors. The script should then automatically come back to you for approval, and most certainly should do so if there are any changes which merely reflect the copy-editor's taste in preference to yours. It is up to you whether you accept such changes. They may well be an improvement, or they may run counter to your own voice and style and therefore jar. Once you have agreed the script, it will in due course go to the printers.

Since here I am concerned with the novel itself, the words, I will not go into matters like publishers' publicity forms, and whether or not you will be consulted over the jacket. Suffice to say that unless your contract states it, you have no rights of consultation over the design aspect of your book.

The next major sign of life as far as the words are concerned should be the arrival of proofs for you to correct. This normally happens between six and nine months after the book is accepted; it could be less, sometimes it is more. Your contract should contain a clause stating that the publishers undertake to issue the book within a certain period, so given that the proofs should have been passed about four months before the end of that period you might contact the publishers if they have not turned up by then.

Don't worry too much if you have not corrected proofs before. *The Writers' & Artists' Yearbook* sets out in detail the way to do it, but if you find all the symbols and squiggles a bit daunting, just try to master the main ones, and make notes on a separate piece of paper concerning any errors you aren't quite sure how to correct. As long as you set these notes out clearly, your publishers should be able to transfer them to the proofs. Do not use this stage as an opportunity to re-write the book — if corrections exceed a certain amount due to your changes of mind you will have to foot the extra typesetting bill. The proofs should also be corrected by both the printers and the publishers.

Novels do not automatically get reviewed. Most genre novels (apart from thrillers and science fiction) are infrequently reviewed in Britain. A conventional first novel might collect a folder of notices or just a couple of mentions in distant provincial papers — or nothing at all. The publishers have no control over this; all they can do is send out the review copies.

How will you react? Will you rush out and buy every paper in hopes, or sit back and wait for any photocopies of reviews to trickle through from the publishers a few weeks after the event? On the whole I think one starts by doing the former and, if one continues to be published, ends up by doing the latter. But I should perhaps confess, and pay a belated thank-you to Monica Foot, that one of the happiest moments of my life occurred on Victoria Station. I had discovered on which days all the newspapers published their book reviews, and I went on the appropriate morning after publication of my first novel to buy a copy of *The Scotsman*, and found that Monica Foot had written some glowing praise which, sixteen years later, I still recall when I pass that particular bookstall.

But one has to remember to keep reviews, particularly unfavourable ones, in perspective. Most of them are — and I say this as someone who has been on the giving as well as the receiving end — pieces of journalism, not considered criticism. You may find you concur with George Eliot who chose not to read her reviews since talk of her books interfered with her writing.

Virginia Woolf understood this: 'I don't take praise or blame excessively to heart, but they interrupt, cast one's eye backwards, make one wish to explain or investigate.'

In fact actual publication can seem very much of an anti-climax. The most exciting part is when the publisher accepts the manuscript. That seems like a threshold into a completely new life. But twelve months later, when the book itself arrives, life has probably not changed a great deal.

'Will you introduce me to Virginia Woolf?' the young Olivia Manning begged her first publisher, who was on the fringe of the Bloomsbury Group. 'Certainly not,' he replied, 'she hates young women writers. She would cut you to pieces.'

Chapter Five

Back to the Beginning

Now let us take things rather more slowly.

You are interested in trying to write a novel, but the flurry of the last two chapters has not been helpful. You need to test your impulses more, and your capabilities. There used to be a London Transport recruitment poster which read, 'When you look in the mirror, do you see a Bus Driver?' You are not at all sure that when you look in the mirror you see a Novelist or are ever likely to. So I am going to examine three questions: What do you like? What do you hate? What do you READ? Your responses may, or may not, illuminate matters a little further.

What do you like?

This sounds rather childish, as though it expects answers like 'chocolate pudding' and 'breaking the ice on puddles', and I don't intend it to be treated as entirely detached from those immediate, certain, childhood likes.

The obvious question – do you like writing? Can you sustain an interest in a piece of your own prose, be it a letter, or an office memorandum, or a piece of fiction? Can you build it, and shape it, and try to make it as sharp as possible? For although one side of writing is the outpouring aspect, the tumble of words that takes you by surprise when you read them back the next day, the obverse side is to do with conscious building: shifting the phrases around, heightening with an adjective here, deleting a superfluous adverb there. As I said in Chapter 3, I found it very difficult to criticise and rewrite my fiction when I first started, but long before that I had taken pleasure in trying to perfect things as dissimilar as poems and committee minutes. I think you must have a feeling of responsibility and challenge as you create your word artefacts.

Fiction can give you unlimited opportunity to indulge the things you like. You may never have the courage to don a hang-gliding harness and jump off Beachy Head, but if you get a thrill from watching others do it (probably on television) you could transfer that excitement to a scene in a novel. 'But I don't have enough imagination to describe what it would really be like.' Then go to a hang-gliding rally and watch closely. William Faulkner said, 'A writer needs three things, experience, observation, and imagination, any two of which, at times any one of which, can supply the lack of others.'

Hang-gliding is an exotic subject; I introduced it to demonstrate that there can be extravagance and indulgence in fiction writing. No need to cast away all your minor caprices as irrelevant to the serious business of writing a novel. For instance I am very fond of the appearance of giraffes, and once wrote a scene in a wild-life park where I introduced a few giraffes into the landscape just for my own pleasure. I had based most of my description on a real park, and when I visited it three years later was disappointed to find there were no giraffes. I had forgotten they were my invention.

What is true for minor caprices is much more true for fundamental preferences and peculiarities. While the construction of a fiction can include elements of daydream, it will have its foundation in your experience and persona. Even deliberate fantasies such as westerns and romances, if they are to have any guts at all, draw on their authors' grasp of character, and that must be based on observation and experience. So it is no use saying your life and personality are too boring to provide material for a novel, no use, that is, if you really intend to write one. You must embrace your loves and your obsessions.

Do you like examining people's behaviour? Trying to work out why X really left her husband, or B decided to give up farming and become a nun? Does the whole sequence of events and emotions that lies behind a statement like 'I can't go home 'cos me dad says I'm a villain' arouse your interest and imagination? Do you enjoy developing a story so that its plot rests securely on credible human behaviour rather than just a series of unusual happenings? Do you like digging beneath the surface of life, get annoyed by the formula-language of the media that reduces tragedies and glories alike to easily-recognised, bite-sized morsels of prose?

When Maureen Duffy was a student she was already writing poetry and plays, but had no special affection for the novel. Then she read James Joyce's *Ulysses* and discovered that 'There was no need it seemed to write a novel in one key or style. And everything could go in: myth, metaphysics, poetry, the insides and outsides of people's heads and guts, sex, religion. It was an enormous liberation.' Can you share that liberation? Not necessarily in conjunction with reading *Ulysses*, but by realising that your passion for hang-gliding, your interest in Aristotle, the mysterious father whom you never knew, the predictable father whom you have known all your life, your asthma, your cat, your music, your aunt's bed-sit, that steamy love affair in Staines, and the accounts department at work, can all end up in the same novel — whose theme, perhaps, is betrayal.

When you sit down to work, don't divorce yourself from yourself in an attempt to become some mythical idea of 'a writer'. Bring everything you know and guess at to your desk. If you like helping to organise conferences, don't dismiss that fact as 'boring'. Isn't what goes on behind the bonhomie and neutrally-worded memoranda of a conference suitable material for fiction? Likewise the private thoughts and visible feelings of half-a-dozen parents as they drive, push, carry, lead or drag their offspring to the same playgroup on a particular October morning?

Human behaviour is the brainfood of most novelists, but some students need a little encouragement before they feel free to operate confidently within the maelstrom of their own accumulated experience.

What do you hate?

This is delicate. Vitriol may not seem the most desirable ink for a novelist's pen. But it cannot be denied that it has inspired some fine writing. Not so much out-and-out hatred of a particular person (see warning on p 34), that would probably result in monotonous work, but hatred of what a person has made you feel. How they have got under your skin, or the emotional damage they have inflicted — however unwittingly — on you, or your family, or your friends.

Many teenagers begin to write out of a feeling of being utterly stifled by their parents and their home surroundings. They don't hate their mothers and fathers, but they hate the constriction of it all: the regular meals, the lavender air freshener in the bathroom, the way the crushed nylon velvet curtains hang. They write to break out into the world.

Their opposites, who have grown up in an atmosphere of uncertainty, may write to create something enduring, something that is entirely their own. Their backgrounds may include so many irregularities and let-downs that they write partly in order to make something coherent and tangible out of it all.

Wider hates against wrongs such as fascism, racism, commercialism, violence or snobbishness, have fuelled much good writing; but they can prove too broad a target for the inexperienced novelist, and may turn what should be a story into a fleshless tract. You need to understand your villains as much as you sympathise with your heroes.

Don't deny your unique hates and frustrations and failures. They are as important as your likes and loves, and pain needs to be illuminated, just as pleasure deserves to be celebrated.

Thus far this chapter may make some of you feel rather as though you have been requested to walk into an unkempt farmyard from which you can expect to emerge with muck on your boots, perhaps a handful of fresh eggs, and possibly a dead fowl which you will have to pluck and draw yourself. But how any of it may bring you nearer to writing a novel remains a mystery.

Well, it is a mystery. And because for many students it is so difficult to find the right opening to the rich path that may lead to a novel, I have been holding the kind of rambling, wayward conversation I would with a student on a writing course, hoping to expose or unite strands of thought which I barely comprehend in a manner which will sometimes suddenly prompt a student to walk thoughtfully away. When next seen he or she will be sitting alone, writing.

What do you read?

There is one way in which a student can annoy me intensely. This is to reply, 'Oh — I don't really know. I can't think of anyone specific just now,' to my question, 'What authors do you like to read?'

If people come on a course with the idea of writing a novel, yet cannot name any author who inspires their interest, my expectations of what they may achieve plummet.

Already some anxious reader will be thinking, 'Oh dear, she expects me to have read all Henry James, George Eliot, Dostoevsky, Flaubert, Theodore Dreiser, Thomas Mann, Virginia Woolf, Hermann Hesse, V.S. Naipaul, Muriel Spark, Alain Robbe-Grillet . . . .' No, no, no, I don't. I just expect you to *read*, and have feelings about what you read.

In an essay John Fowles admitted that 'My lack of decent reading has become increasingly embarrassing. I am faced with it every time I meet students, and the vast uncharted spaces in my knowledge of the contemporary — and the classical — novel are revealed', but then went on to describe with relish the books that do absorb him — descriptions of old trials, travel books, historical memoirs, anything that will 'give me the sharp feel of the age it was written in'.

Any would-be novelist must, I feel, identify to some extent with the feeling of discovery Alan Sillitoe had as a boy when he went to a public library. 'The first time I went in I couldn't believe that so many books were free — at my disposal. I was astonished to see hundreds of clean and neatly stacked books, a catalogued treasure-house of handy volumes waiting to be borrowed three at a time.'

The fact that he had failed to win a scholarship to grammar school no longer mattered 'with so much knowledge free for all'.

The best way to find out how novels are written is to read them. As Edward Young remarked two centuries ago, 'It is by a sort of noble contagion, from a general familiarity with their writings, and not by any particular sordid theft, that we can be the better for those who went before us.'

Some people are directly motivated to write by what they read. They want to create a throng of characters like Iris Murdoch does, or reconstruct their painful youth like Jean Rhys, or explore the society and region from which they come like Melvyn Bragg. Others want to tackle a certain subject more fully, or more truthfully, than they feel any other author has done. Chinua Achebe, the Nigerian novelist, described in an interview how he was prompted to begin: 'I was quite certain that I was going to try my hand at writing, and one of the things that set me thinking was Joyce Cary's novel set in Nigeria . . . which was praised so much, and it was clear to me that this was a most superficial picture of — not only of the country, but even of the Nigerian character and so I thought if this was famous, then perhaps someone ought to try and look at this from the inside.'

That is a wholly honourable motivation. The sort of comment I mistrust is when someone says, 'This book's a load of rubbish, I could write a better one,' in the tones of the ignorant, bewildered, and therefore angry parent who claims their child paints better than Picasso. The student who can experience the sensation described by Bamber Gascoigne as that 'miraculous late-for-meals long-on-the-lavatory seized-by-a-book feeling' will get far more from their reading than the easily-irked student, anxious to belittle.

I expect most people will find it difficult to believe that students turn up on writing courses who are not already avid readers. I find it difficult myself, but it is a fact. Rather than their general apathy I would really sooner encounter an Uncle Matthew (from Nancy Mitford's *The Pursuit of Love*) who said: 'I have only ever read one book in my life, and that is *White Fang.* It's so frightfully good I've never bothered to read another.' At least that demonstrates a capacity for enthusiasm.

Chapter Six

Grandmothers and Paragraphs

The title of this chapter refers to teaching approaches used by two writers I have tutored fiction courses with at the Arvon Foundation centres in West Yorkshire and Devon. They are Colin Spencer and David Plante, brilliant novelists both, in completely contrasting guises.

Usually (though by no means always) students who come on fiction courses have not actually finished a novel, and are unlikely even to have started one. They are there to find out how they might begin, whether they show any potential, and to share five days' life, work and conversation with fellow-aspirants and two professionals.

When everyone gathers together on the first evening it is impossible to predict what will unfold. (I once made the mistake of deciding that of the dozen or so people I was meeting for the first time, there was just one who might find it difficult to gather enough confidence to write fiction. He was in the army, about twenty, and very shy. It turned out, however, that he had brought with him the manuscripts of two competently-written novels and was half-way through his third!)

Given, then, that the majority of students are tentatively feeling their way, it is necessary on a short course to find a working method that unites them loosely as a group but does not curb their initiative.

Colin Spencer, whose sequence of novels *Generation* explores the complex emotional lives of a family over three generations, encourages students to strip away pre-conceived ideas about 'creative writing' and concentrate on their own experience. He is a truth-seeker, and knows that writers cannot hide behind self-deception and pretty words.

We agreed that after we had talked to each student individually, finding out what writing they had done and what they hoped to achieve from the course, we would ask them to write a description of a person whom they knew really well. This, Colin explained to them, was not to be a flat, school-essay type of description, but something vivid, personal and original. When we read it, we were to get the taste, the feel, the image of that person.

This raised some questions. Did it *have* to be someone they knew terribly well? Most people don't want to write about their husbands, or mothers, or lovers, or at least not if they are to be as expressive and honest as we had asked.

In the discussion that followed, Colin suggested they might depict one of their grandparents, since sometimes there is a combination of detachment and intimacy in our relationship with our grandparents that makes it comparatively easy to write about them. But, of course, they could choose absolutely anybody.

'And,' said one student, 'you won't know if they're real or if we made them up.'

'Exactly,' we replied.

'But,' said another, bewildered, 'you said we should write a description of someone we know really well.'

'But you can know someone who doesn't exist very well indeed,' retorted the first student. 'Think of Heathcliff – or Winnie-the-Pooh.'

It turned out that several people drew on their grandmothers, though they did not always make it evident. One student wrote about a young wife, and another about a stranger moving into the house next door, and then both later admitted that the characters were based on their grandmothers. They had begun to experience the way imagination and reality merge.

Students worked at their own pace and in their own manner. One or two shut themselves away for hours, emerging only when they had completed the description to the best of their ability. Others brought their work to us at every stage of its development. Some showed their drafts to one another for mutual criticism. Everyone tried to have something sufficiently complete to read out when we gathered together after supper.

The time limitation meant that most students learned that they must select only the information that would be completely relevant to the shape and feel and length of their piece. If they had a gap in their knowledge they had to invent, supplying mortar from their imagination to make a whole from the separate bricks of fact and observation which were lodged in their memory.

Hemingway explains the process like this: 'A writer, if he is any good, does not describe. He invents or *makes* out of knowledge personal and impersonal and sometimes he seems to have unexplained knowledge which could come from forgotten racial or family experience.'

Although we had used the word 'describe' when asking the students to write about a person, I in fact agree with Hemingway that 'make' is more appropriate — but one needs experience of the process to realise this. A student asked to 'make' a character in words might be baffled. Yet writing fiction has something in common with the building up of a sculpture, flake by flake, from an amorphous mound of clay.

By showing work in its early stages to Colin and me, some students realised more quickly than they might have done on their own what it really means when one says: 'Remember! The reader has only the words on the page to draw on. He doesn't have the additional memory, the actual experience and feeling which those words are supposed to represent. Try to put yourself in the reader's place. Will you hold his interest and his understanding? Have you transplanted the experience, the image, from your mind to his through the medium of words?' And the fact that we sometimes reacted quite differently to a piece of work might momentarily have confused a student, but it also began to illustrate the complexity that can exist in the creation of just a single character.

Because we had time to talk about each student's work, and about our own methods of writing, we were able to convince everyone that there is no clear-cut answer to the question: 'Do you base your characters on people you know?' Some do more than others, but it isn't like taking a photograph or reporting for a newspaper.

E.M. Forster said that 'A useful trick is to look back upon a person with half-closed eyes, fully describing certain characteristics. A likeness isn't aimed at and couldn't be obtained, because a man's only himself amidst the particular circumstances of his life.' In other words, as soon as you appropriate a person for your novel, giving him things to do and words to speak, he is your character, not the Mr Smith down the road who inspired him.

Joyce Cary answered the question by saying, 'Never, you can't. You may get single hints. But real people are too complex and too disorganised for books.' I think Colin Spencer would disagree with that. He tries to include the complexity and the disorganisation because they are the truth. But inevitably, as he looks hard at real life, it condenses, and, like the sculptor, he separates flakes from that compression and builds them into a story with shape and sense; a story which could not have existed without either the actual experience of his life or the subsequent application of his mind and imagination.

On the morning after the students had completed their construction of a character, Colin asked them to start something quite separate. This time they were to write about a place. Again the writing must be sharp. Readable for its own sake, as well as evoking a room, or a field, or a street, or an ocean. Whatever they liked.

In a way, this sounded easier. But as they came to us throughout the day some of them bemoaned that they found it more difficult. A person, when you tried to recreate and/or invent them, often forced their individuality into the words. But a place just sat there, waiting; defying you to reduce its multiformity to a few paragraphs. And they already knew the dangers, from previous discussions, of lapsing into purple adjectival prose.

'Why,' I asked tentatively, when one student had rewritten a dull description of a dull, nettly yard for the third time, 'did you choose this place?'

'Oh . . . well. Because I was sitting in it when someone down the road hanged himself.'

'Did you know he was hanging himself?'

'Oh no. I was only five. I sort of found out. Later. And worked out I'd been sitting in the yard at the time.'

'Could you get some of that atmosphere into it? Without actually mentioning the hanging. Abstract it somehow?'

'I'll try.'

He wrote a very good, sombre paragraph. The place, with its nettles and broken shed and rusty machinery now seemed to exude an atmosphere of death and dread, without those actual words being used.

'You didn't include these rusty machines earlier,' I said. 'They're good. Have you just remembered them?'

'No. I invented them. Well . . . that's not true. I've shifted them half a mile. They used to be piled outside the old farm down the road.'

At this stage in the course two or three of the students were becoming preoccupied. They joined in the session after supper when again everyone read out their pieces, but they were not completely involved. Their minds were beginning to explore territory that two days' writing and discussion had begun to reveal.

'Are you going to set us something specific tomorrow?'

'Is there something *you* want to do?'

'Well — yes, there is rather.'

'Then do it. Tomorrow's suggestion is only for those who want to take it up.'

Tomorrow's suggestion was this. You've created a person and you've created a place. Now put them together in a piece of fiction.

It didn't work for everybody, but we could see private expressions of concentration or even glee on other students' faces.

For some the liaison came naturally. Although their people and places had had no deliberate connection, they were drawn from a close personal territory within which links were easy to make. But for one student a feasible link appeared to be out of the question. He had written about his grandmother when she was dying in hospital, and the Mont Ste-Victoire in Provence which Cézanne so often painted. But he faced the challenge with relish and imagination.

Now here I must break off to explain that although in the context of the particular course I am describing the immediate result of bringing together a person and a place could obviously at most be a short story and not a novel, I am nevertheless not in this book talking about short stories. Their omission may be a little difficult to understand.

Many novelists do of course write short stories, but I want here to concentrate on the stamina required for a novel; to persuade students to pace themselves for a marathon rather than a sprint.

'So why do you require students to assemble elements that might make a short story but could not make a novel?'

Well, they could not make a complete novel, but they might constitute parts of one. And the object of the exercise was to ease students into the processes of fiction. If the result, for some, was a short story, that is admirable. But my focus here is on the novel.

'Why don't you devote just a section of this book to the short story?'

Because it shouldn't be crammed into 'just a section'. It's too special, too important.

'But I want to start with short stories. Before I begin to think about tackling a novel.'

Fine. That is how many people begin. Perhaps I should warn you however that in my experience they're more difficult to write than novels. Just as poems are more difficult to write than short stories. Write well, that is. Obviously in terms of effort a bad short poem is less exacting than a bad novel.

Do you remember Henry James saying that the novel 'will stretch anywhere — it will take in absolutely anything'? And Maureen Duffy saying 'everything could go in: myth, metaphysics, poetry, the insides and outsides of people's heads and guts, sex, religion'? That is the realisation I want this book to carry. All embracing, liberating — and sometimes untidy too.

But not sloppy. Which brings me to paragraphs and David Plante.

David has a soft American voice which makes the word 'paragraph' sound both mysterious and like a caress. I have regarded it in a different light since we did a fiction course together — no longer a straightforward chunk of prose, but an entity of infinite potential.

After we had talked to each student individually, he told them he wanted them to go away and write a single paragraph.

'What about?'

Anything. Anything in the world. But it must be a *good* paragraph. As perfect as they could make it.

Now if it had been a poetry course, and 'poem' had been substituted for 'paragraph', the students would not have been taken aback. But few of them were aware that one can write a paragraph and subject it to as much rigorous care and criticism as you can a sonnet.

It was difficult for some of them at first. The paragraph, whether it was descriptive or contained some action, seemed to hang there, lifeless, gasping for a context.

But David showed how the nuances, the word order, the colour, the rhythm, the sound, could all be scrutinised and combed and improved, until the paragraph attained its own modest structure and independence.

This exercise brought the students right up against the rock face of prose creation. And as one discussed the subtle difference of meaning or effect between one phrase and another, a new territory began to reveal itself to some of them. They began to discover the abstract essence of prose; to be watchful and patient, and to take responsibility for every mark they made. One student became so obsessed by his paragraph that he rewrote it fifty-three times during the course. Other students continued with the exercise for a couple of days, starting new paragraphs from time to time, and then launched into longer pieces of fiction with heightened awareness.

Some readers may feel this is a very clinical exercise. In fact, as conducted by David Plante, it is quite the opposite. He treats every sentence with intimacy rather than precept. He once wrote:

> I don't have an analytical mind. This sometimes worries me and makes me envious of other people's power of analysis. By necessity, I must make an advantage of what may be a weakness: my intuitive faith, based, I think, in a *sense* of what I want to write, a sense I never quite succeed in realising. It is what is left out of writing, what writing can't state, which possesses me — certain senses, certain states of consciousness, as real to us as eating and sleeping and working. They are inarticulate, but distinct and powerful. Above all, they are *ordinary*. They are the substance of my work, and my effort is to make them rich and dense.

And by encouraging students to be intimate with their words, he teaches them to explore nebulous states of consciousness which are as much part of fiction as the social observation of a Dickens.

I learned something valuable from listening to what he said about his own work and that of the students. This was to add 'paragraphs' to the jumble of notes that I push into a folder when a new novel is germinating. I don't usually keep a notebook because I find retrieving observations and information from a bound journal rather cumbersome. But I do write things down on separate pieces of paper and then when I want to start work on a novel I can flip through the sheets, throw away any that seem irrelevant, and sort the others according to their applicability to characters or particular sections of the book.

Usually they are rather cryptic messages. These examples are taken at random from my current folder:

> The five tulips — red/vermilion/(pink) in red Venetian jug, slightly painterly surface, verging orange. Sometimes she felt her colour-observation/use had become ossified. Like a writer who can only find the same words to use.
>
> Quite separate from family and video, he will have girls in the town. Going out to them on cold clear nights.
>
> My father was 6′ tall and whenever I needed to visualize a measurement like 12′ for the width of a carpet or a road, I would see my father duplicated on the floor.
>
> Jos did not like to get to know people too well, see them too often; for then the circumspect image they presented to the world began to split and waver, and she got more and more glimpses of the uncertainties underneath.
>
> In the new surroundings — ? bright light, sharp verticals & horizontals, desert — the clarity of the death pill kept by one citizen in a secret hiding place.
>
> Someone whose madness is starting to plan menus to cover the rest of their life.

I have learned over the years how valuable these cryptic messages can be. Occasionally their essence leaks away after a short passage of time, but more often than not they contribute to the intensity and diversity of a book. Being short on imagination I find I cannot create satisfactory fiction straight from my head over a continuous period of a few months; I need these messages to accumulate until they form a kind of organic jig-saw, waiting to be assembled.

And to the messages I have now added paragraphs. Occasionally, when I have a particularly evocative observation which I want to preserve, I don't just scribble it down with careless brevity, but I write it as a considered paragraph. This means that when the folder is examined and the real work begins, I find a few completed items among the raw stock. This is a great encouragement, since too many after-wine jottings like 'To wake up dead would be marvellous: to wake up as one of 5,000 angels on a pinhead' can be irritating on a cold Monday morning, but they fall into perspective beside a few properly nurtured paragraphs.

These two paragraphs grew out of a simple observation of the noises in a small house which I turned into a minor piece of action for my intended two main characters:

> After five minutes Pete switched off everything in the room that was making a noise: the video from Kristie which had been delivered overnight, the desk-lamp which made a faint hum, and the refrigerator. Outside the starlings squealed. In between their cries he listened for Jos. Was she working or was she still sitting at the breakfast table?
>
> As soon as he had left the kitchen, Jos had moved from the table to the window. Then she waited for the moment when he tried to hear what she was doing. She heard him cross the floor, and noted the cessation of the video. She held her breath. She would not even give him the information that she was still alive.

Of course I may not in the end be able to use them, but at the moment these short paragraphs provide a flake of solid flesh for the story in my head. Though I am afraid they are prosaic Kitchen paragraphs, nothing spellbinding; but one has to learn to recognise the sound of one's own voice.

Chapter Seven

Opinions and Participation

Because of my wish to lead nervous students straight into fiction rather than leave them shivering on the brink, I am now guilty of hovering on a particular brink myself. That is of facing up to the fact that some of you will still be very unsure whether your writing has any strength or quality, and will be uncertain how it may be improved. This will perhaps particularly apply to those who were not 'good' at English at school and who are diffident about their ability ever to write well.

One of the reasons I wanted to encourage students to leap into the experience of fiction was that some find, when they begin to write out at length, that they have a natural 'voice', with or without academic achievements. True, their writing may need correction and polishing, but that is easier to tackle when you have the confidence created by the completion of a sizeable chunk of prose.

But how about those who are still very critical of the quality of their attempts? Who can see for themselves that the sentences are lacklustre, and would prefer to eradicate whatever 'voice' they can detect since it sounds more like the voice of incompetence than anything else? They know that practice, and more practice, is the daily medicine, but want to develop their own critical powers.

Then I would ask that they seek out, if they have not already done so, the first book in this series. Called *The Way to Write*, it is about the effective use of language – and how formal, and therefore inapplicable, *that* phrase sounds. In fact it is a very personal book, full of insights and splendour, by John Fairfax and John Moat who founded the Arvon centres at which the courses described in the previous chapter were held. In it they explore the magic as well as the nuts and bolts of writing, so that inspiration and syntax are not segregated.

Here they are at their most practical:

> There's nothing that sooner reveals a writer's skill, or lack of it, than his use of the adjective. The bad writer simply cannot hear

when the adjective is contributing to, as opposed to compromising or merely duplicating, the meaning of a noun. He writes of 'lovely roses' and 'useful utensils', and of 'millipedes with countless legs'. With adjectives he either states the obvious, or else puts truth out of focus.

But used by a fine writer the adjective is a word of unrivalled delight. It is adornment, the jewellery, the leaves on the tree. It brings the picture into exact focus; or in other words it focuses the reader's eye exactly as the writer wishes.

And alongside they give this quotation by Sir Ernest Gower:

If we make a habit of saying 'The true facts are these', we shall come under suspicion when we profess to tell merely 'the facts'.

And here, under the heading *Sound,* they have this lovely paragraph:

If you recite aloud the five vowels, A E I O U, you do something in a sense similar to painting on a piece of paper the seven colours of the spectrum. You mark the cardinal points in a circle of possibility.

If you want to learn more about the components and potentiality of our language, then please read their book. I think it should help you scrutinise your writing from many different angles, and it may immediately pinpoint the bad habits and illuminate good ones.

But a brief warning. In my experience it is often the quite accomplished writers who feel certain that their work is inadequate and tend to be over-critical, while the leaden-footed ones go blithely on, confident they are achieving something.

While trying to develop a basic sense that tells you whether or not a piece of writing is satisfactory, it is also important to find a voice, a tone, with which you feel comfortable. Don't adopt a formal, or a racy, or an elaborate, or an aggressive tone just because you think it is appropriate to the subject you have chosen. (Though, of course, if you can sustain that tone without strain, and find it effective, then by all means go ahead.) The inexplicable goal is to discover a way of writing in which your intellect merges with your feelings. This means that the action and ideas in the story are clearly expressed, but they do not stand awkwardly against the personal chemistry which dictates the rhythms and colour of your prose. As in any complex activity, you need to be aware of what you are doing most of the time, but you also need to learn to trust your impulses. Anthony Burgess has written that in his experience the bulk of the work of writing novels for adults 'is done at the preconscious level' but also 'some kind of control is exerted by the conscious — the shaping mind, as it is called . . .'.

Now, let us suppose that you have gone as far as you can on your own. You may have a folder of unconnected pieces; you may have a complete novel which has been rejected by a few publishers. Some people at this stage, rather than seek criticism by showing and sharing their work, may prefer just to let it be. For the moment at any rate.

I quite understand that feeling. Writing is very private, and it is possible to break into that privacy to no good purpose.

But if you feel you could show it to someone, would like to take the risk or even positively welcome the risk, then what are your options?

There are friends; there are relations; there are people like teachers who might be expected to have an informed opinion. Only you can decide whether you think they are likely to be objective and helpful; and only you can decide whether you are prepared to listen to their opinions without getting upset. There is just one suggestion I would make: don't show your work to friends simply in the hope of praise. I know we all need praise, but we also need criticism. And don't decide after showing your work and receiving less than acclaim, that the reader is too thick to understand what you are trying to do anyway. If you really believe that, then don't ask for their opinion in the first place.

Entwined with the whole complication of showing work to friends and relatives is fear of their trying to identify events and descriptions in the book with incidents in your own life. This is more of a poser than some people may realise. I talked earlier about Colin Spencer's series of novels *Generation.* It is not, could not be, a precise photographic record of his experiences within a particular family, but neither could *Generation* have existed in its present form without that family. But some people simply cannot write out their most intense experiences, even though they may be expressed through fictitious characters, if they feel their writing will shock, hurt, or vicariously intrigue those who are close to them.

I know no direct way out of this tangle. On the whole, rather than stop writing or blunt your work by too much discretion and cottonwool, I suggest a certain aloofness. Don't show your novel to your nearest and dearest, or encourage too much interest, and if it does ever get published . . . well, by then it's a *fait accompli*, and people will probably be as much intrigued by the mere fact of publication as by the actual content of the book.

I am though assuming that you are making *fiction* out of your experience, and not using writing simply as a means of slagging off people who have discomfited you. You should remember that there is an enforceable law of libel, the main principles of which are described in *The Writers' & Artists' Yearbook*. Basically it is against the law to publish something which contains recognisably defamatory information about a particular person — ie information which lowers that person's position in, or acceptance by, society. It is not a law which is very often enforced, but do bear it in mind and act responsibly. If one of your minor characters is partly based on half-Polish Jacob Street who has a finger missing on his left hand and was found not guilty on a charge of grievous bodily harm, then don't turn him into quarter-Polish Jacob Greet who has a finger missing on his right hand and was found guilty on a charge of manslaughter.

In many districts there are writing groups, often run independently, sometimes under the auspices of the local authority or regional arts association. These can be a way of meeting local writers, and of discovering what effect your work has on others. Beware though of the partisanship of such a group, for sometimes their members are too kindly to express anything other than praise and encouragement to fellow aspirants. I have attended one or two, and although I understand *why* there were cries of, 'Oh, well done Jim; that was really moving!' after diffident Jim had stumbled through a very muddled story, I didn't feel it was going to help him much when the initial enthusiasm was not followed by a little constructive criticism.

For many people, however, a self-help writing group may be all that is available for local writers. But it is worth asking your regional arts association or local public library whether they know of any courses or lectures or readings that might be of interest to you. And if you live within reach of an institution that holds evening and part-time classes, then find out whether they include writing on their syllabus. London is well-served: The City Literary Institute and Morley College in particular run a range of excellent writing classes. Community arts centres, both in London and elsewhere, quite often include writing among their projects.

Remember, though, that tutors who take fiction classes don't normally run an extensive reading service as well. They will talk about the work you read out in class, or any pieces they have particularly asked to see, but they cannot be expected to take home armfuls of students' novels and produce reports on them. The simple reason for this is that they are paid only for the few hours they teach and not for any out-of-class work — and reading a novel can take several hours.

So what about these Arvon Centres you were talking about earlier? you may ask. Would it be worth my taking five days out of my life to go to one? It might be.

The foreword by Ted Hughes to John Fairfax and John Moat's

book tells how he was at first completely dismissive of the venture, but then gradually became wholeheartedly involved. It is a closely argued, passionate testimony on behalf of the Arvon method. Read it, and find out if it strikes a chord.

In that foreword, Ted Hughes talks about the English attitude during the Sixties which ridiculed the whole idea of teaching creative writing — usually citing the American experience as supposedly good evidence for such scorn. But in fact, as he points out, many of the best American writers have attended and/or taught writing classes, and if Arvon has achieved one thing it is to show hundreds of British writers who have tutored their courses that such teaching can be rewarding in manifold and unexpected ways. Apart from anything else, it means that two writers who might otherwise never have met, can exchange ideas and experiences and get an insight into one another's work.

I would like to include here a mention of my earliest exploration into the need for a more sympathetic approach to creative writing teaching in England. In 1963, when Ann Quin and I had both been working for several years in administrative jobs in art schools, we became rather fed up with the fact that most of each working day was spent nannying painting students much the same age as ourselves who had local authority grants, leaving us only the evenings for our own work. So we decided to send a proposal to selected eminent writers to find out whether they would support the idea of a writing school, and then, if they were encouraging, we would organise a committee 'to try to thrash out some proposals which could be set down in a report to submit to the government.' Not surprisingly, we did not get very far with our rather grandiose scheme, though the now-yellowed folder labelled 'WRITING SCHOOL' includes friendly letters from Angus Wilson and Robert Graves — and Richard Crossman, since it seemed likely he would soon become Minister of Education. Robert Graves's letter, while by no means giving instant support to the idea, contains this statement:

> Though whatever can restore the national conscience about clear, economical, vigorous English (which got mislaid when typewriters came into general use) has my ardent good wishes . . .

And the foreword by Ted Hughes, referred to above, includes this:

> Whatever happens on these courses . . . the actual hour-by-hour work is mainly a business of scrutinising language in action, a laborious business of discrimination and definition, fitting words to one precise purpose or another.
>
> And this is an activity which can be exercised anywhere, in a classroom or in private. It does not need the special circumstances of

an Arvon course to justify its usefulness.

If we were a healthy society, presumably we would not need to be schooled so deliberately into an understanding of the life of our own language — our society itself would supply the understanding naturally and fully, in the flourishing use of our mother-tongue. But we have to admit our society fails there. ...... It seems to me we now have to regard the body of our language as we might regard the body of a man in prison: only a deliberate regimen of planned exercise will keep it going at all, let alone develop athletic prowess.

The full-time writing school idea, I now believe, was not a good one, growing as it did partly out of envy; but what I think is shared by Robert Graves, Ted Hughes, John Moat, John Fairfax, Ann Quin and myself, and, judging by their response to Arvon, many other writers, is a wish that the 'national conscience' might be invigorated as far as effective writing is concerned. And the experience of sharing, the gathering together of two or three — or twenty or thirty — can help to achieve this.

Chapter Eight

Types of Novel

I wonder what you have in mind when you say 'the novel'? It might be the English heritage that includes Austen, Eliot, Hardy and Lawrence. It might be something more quixotic — Sterne, Joyce, Beckett, Nye. It might be anything that would satisfy John Fowles when he says, 'I also hate books that can be put down; and if they have no narrative to sustain them then they had better, so far as I am concerned, be bloody good in other directions.' Or your preference might be for something that can be classified under headings such as Thriller, Occult, Western, Romance or Science Fiction.

At this point perhaps some of you are going to start getting interested for the first time. 'Oh good. I thought she'd never stop going on about that boring dredging up of personal experience stuff.' And others are going to think, 'Oh surely she doesn't really take that kind of pop pulp stuff seriously?' To the latter I would say: Have you ever read Patricia Highsmith, Stephen King, Ray Bradbury, John Le Carré, Reginald Hill or Ursula Le Guin, all of whom may be shelved in shops under categories, and all of whom write as well as many of the authors who have been short-listed for the prestigious annual Booker literary prize? Which is not to say badly-written category novels are not published, they are. But there are mediocre and boring conventional novels published too.

Kingsley Amis is of the opinion that the best genre writers 'move on a level of sophistication and insight that the standard modern novel aspires to without reaching'. Too often, he believes, the standard novel nowadays 'is a self-indulgent moan, a hunk of life neither well-observed nor presented in any style, a glum ideological fantasy.' William Golding is not so welcoming to the genre novel. But over twenty years ago he prophesied that 'Writers who aim at selling their work — surely a minimal dignity to hope for — will be forced more and more to conform to stereotyped patterns . . .' Through his experience as a teacher he had learned that boys 'divide books into categories. There are sexy books, war books, westerns, travel books, science fiction. A boy will accept anything from a section he knows rather than risk another sort.'

Many novelists prefer to work within a category, and many have been faced with the choice of either writing category fiction in addition to their standard fiction or finding work other than writing in order to survive. Some find a freedom, a release of the imagination, as they explore these new territories; others find they get stuck on a treadmill.

While it is true that there is a hungrier market for category fiction than for the standard novel, I don't think it is a good idea to force yourself into a genre if it makes you uncomfortable. To begin with, the important thing is to discover your own fictional territory.

But there may come a time when you would like to try your hand at, say, a thriller, especially if you yourself have always found them good entertainment. Before plunging into your story, do some market research. Go to a well-stocked paperback thriller section in a shop and pick out two or three which you either know have been successful or which look interesting. Read them, this time not for pure escapism, but with a watchful eye. What seems to be the ingredients that make them work?

Often you will find that in good category fiction the right ingredients are exactly the same as in a standard novel: credible characters, convincing dialogue, vivid descriptions of place. But you will also discover the importance of the pacing of a story. The shocks and reversals don't happen all in one chapter, leaving acres of flat exposition. A good narrative gradually builds and builds, carrying you along with it, and keeping all the varying tensions and developments carefully balanced.

If some of the books you pick up seem rather rubbishy, don't try to emulate them — aim to do better. But you might try to guess what makes them popular. They may plot a story well despite impoverished prose, or they may have a glamorous background to attract readers, or they may be cashing in on a currently fashionable theme. Sometimes one can use a blatantly popular ingredient to embellish a sound, well-crafted book.

Above all you must remember that regular genre readers have expectations. They don't want to spend their money only to find that a book cheats within its type.

For example, a 'frightener' must *be* frightening. This requires extremely careful construction and rich descriptive writing. It isn't enough to read a newspaper report about an alleged haunted house where the walls in one room bleed, and just plonk that incident into a book and have one character after another being frightened by it. You have got to create an imaginative context for the bleeding wall so that even the most sceptical reader does not doubt its power.

And if you attempt a whodunnit type of thriller, then you have the difficult task of both keeping your reader guessing right up to the end, and making sure that all the characters are behaving credibly. Also the denouement has got to be *interesting.* If the murderer turns out to be a very minor character who hasn't appeared since page four, your reader is likely to feel very let down.

In a crime novel which is not the whodunnit type but a realistic portrayal of a murder, then the reader needs to feel involved with the crime and find it believable. The mere fact of a killing is not enough to turn a poor standard novel into an acceptable crime novel; the web of action and motive that leads to the murder must be exciting or painful or tragic — or preferably exciting *and* painful *and* tragic.

In any type of suspense fiction — and really all category novels have an element of suspense, be it attached to ghosts, murder, spy rings or does-she-marry-the-duke? — the mechanics of the plot shouldn't be heard to creak. You must be fully in control of your story, expressing it through action, natural dialogue and subtle observation, never through clumsy coincidences and exposition. (Not all coincidences, of course, are clumsy; some are exquisitely exciting.) The moments at which you reveal your information must not appear to have been chosen arbitrarily. It is no good having a major climax which depends on a piece of hitherto concealed information if the reader can see no logical reason why the information could not have been made known in Chapter One. There has got to be a narrative truth, and a psychological truth, within the fibre of the most fantastical of stories if it is to qualify as an original novel and not just mechanical formula-writing.

My own view is that good characterisation is the greatest benefit a 'straight' novelist can bring to category fiction. Science-fiction, for example, with a number of honourable exceptions, has suffered from writers who are expert at invention but seem simply to lack interest in the people who inhabit their imagined planets and machines. This tends to alienate unscientific readers who would be quite happy to follow any story if only they were interested in the leading characters.

Specialist knowledge of a particular background can be of immense use in category fiction. This is obvious in fields such as war adventure, police thrillers, spy stories or hospital romance. Sometimes it is less obvious. While, for example, you may feel no desire to use your knowledge of the wholesale fruit and vegetable market at Nine Elms in a standard novel about a divorcing couple, it could be very useful as a background in a murder story. And many people do enjoy reading inside descriptions of the workings of special communities. Magazine offices, auctioneers, harbours, model agencies, television studios, oil rigs, medical schools, horse trials, trade unions, finishing schools — there are thousands of diverse worlds in which murders could be committed, or lifts jam for no apparent mechanical reaon, or space creatures appear.

But remember! A mere listing of the appurtenants of one of those worlds will have your reader asleep in two minutes. That world needs to be integral to the action just as much in a genre novel as was, say, farming in Hardy's novels.

There is usually one student in each fiction class who, when discussion turns to backgrounds, says anxiously, 'Do you have to do a lot of research?' The word 'research' seems to daunt them in extreme.

Well, you don't *have* to do anything; you don't *have* to write a novel. How much research does your book need?

If you read widely, have a good memory and a rich imagination, it would be quite possible to write a light historical romance that had no pretentions to complete period verisimilitude with just a modicum of research. This does not mean you insult your readers with wrong information, but that you concentrate on relationships and atmosphere rather than a finely-etched social background. If, however, you were planning to write a war adventure set in Paris in 1916 and have little knowledge of the First World War and less of France, presumably you would have to do a great deal of research.

It would, I think, be unwise to embark on a first novel which needed a lot of very fundamental research, particularly if you have no experience of integrating learned (as opposed to experienced) facts into creative writing. It is all too easy to get bogged down in detail, and all too difficult to make your characters move and breathe amid your amassed pieces of evidence.

But on the other hand it is sloppy to gloss over some scene just because you are too lazy to go to the library to look up information like the effects of arsenic, or the gestatory period of cats, or the symptoms of mumps, or the school-leaving age in 1939. If you are unused to ferreting out facts, the staff in the reference section of a public library will advise you. Do seek their help, because there is nothing more frustrating than being surrounded by books yet not knowing where to look for answers to your queries. And, obversely, it is extremely satisfying to become familiar with the stock and layout of a library so that you can find your way easily into diverse realms of information.

One of the advantages of getting older is that one's own collection of books grows, and increasingly the answer to a query may lie on one's own shelves. Certainly I think it is wise to build up a selection of reference books — many are published in paperback and they are great time-savers.

Be commonsensical about research. If, like my fictional lover of hang-gliding in Chapter 5, you are rather short on imagination, then increasing your own experience of places and events, and making notes, will enrich your choice of settings.

And if you are already interested in, say, old folk rituals, then you might find them a good ingredient for an occult chiller and would enjoy finding out more of their history. But remember — an occult chiller is no place for dry exposition.

There is a danger attached to research. If you like doing it, then it is easy to kid yourself that you are 'working' while buried in a library, when perhaps all you are really doing is escaping from writing. (I speak from experience!)

I will try to demonstrate with an extract from my last novel how research, imagination and experience can merge. It was in fact my first venture into genre fiction and is an historical novel based on the life of Lizzy Siddall, the model who married the pre-Raphaelite painter, Dante Gabriel Rossetti. The lives of the famous members of that circle — Millais, Ruskin, Morris, etc — are heavily documented, but by comparison really very little is known about Lizzy.

The first picture she posed for, when she was sixteen and working long hours in a milliner's shop, was a scene from *Twelfth Night* painted by Walter Deverell. I had a small reproduction of the painting to look at, and information about Deverell's appearance and manner, but I knew nothing at all about how Lizzy reacted during her first experience as an artist's model. So I looked carefully at the clothes she was wearing in the picture, read the appropriate scene in the play, and drew on my own experience of artists' studios. The scene starts with Walter speaking to Lizzy.

> 'Now here is where you may change. I do hope you will find the clothes comfortable. It is the part where Viola is dressed as a young man, a page, in the court of Duke Orsino. When she is searching for her brother. And Feste, the jester, comes to sing to the Duke. And you, Viola, lean forward, and listen, and watch the Duke's sadness and yearn. Because, as you know, you are in love with him, and he is in love with Olivia.'
>
> Lizzy, who didn't know at all, said nothing, but went into the room, closed the door, and regarded the pile of clothes on the chair. There was a long tunic with double sleeves — tight inner ones, and split, loose outer ones — pale woollen tights, and long pointed leather shoes. They seemed clean, but faintly musty. How could a girl wear such clothes when she was in love with a duke?
>
> When she realised how much her legs were revealed below the

tunic, she panicked. Not so much from modesty, as the fact that her knees and calves were quite solid in comparison to the rest of her body. Walter Deverell would take one look at her and send her straight back home. She walked over to the window, her heart thumping, and gripped the sill. The river beyond the trees glinted like pewter. She wished she could drown.

She stayed like that until there was a gentle tap at the door. 'Miss Siddall? Miss Siddall?'

She did not reply.

'Miss Sid?'

The sound of his voice using her nickname made her feel even more desperate.

'Miss Sid? Are you changed?'

Despairingly she murmured 'Yes' and very quietly and carefully he opened the door. She did not turn to face him, and remained by the window.

'That is perfect,' he said. 'Quite perfect.' He took a few steps into the room. 'Please come next door into the studio.'

She still could not look him in the face. 'I feel . . . foolish.'

'No. It's the rest of the world that's foolish, because they aren't dressed for the Illyrian court. Please come and let me show you what to do.'

She followed him into a high studio lit from skylights in the ceiling, and containing a miscellaneous clutter of brushes, jars of colour and chemicals, stacked canvases, old pieces of furniture, treasured objects, flowers long dead, and a heavy easel which seemed to dominate the silent room.

The easel held a large rectangular canvas, in the background of which steps and balustrades and courtiers and trees collided in a mysterious perspective. In the foreground, on a tiled courtyard, boy musicians played to a heavy young man in rich medieval dress who lolled in a seat at the base of a pillar. On either side of him were shadowy sketches of figures. The one on the left, Walter explained, was to be Viola, sitting on the edge of a bench, facing the duke and gazing up at his face. While the figure on a box on the duke's right was the jester, Feste, who was singing the song that was making the duke stare into the middle distance in such a melancholy fashion.

'My friend Gabriel Rossetti has agreed to sit for Feste,' said Walter with a touch of importance.

Lizzy scrutinized the face of the duke and decided it would be difficult for anyone to feel besotted by him. But she obediently sat exactly where she was told, arranging her feet and clasping her hands as directed, and found a position for her body which she could hold without too much difficulty. When Walter asked if he could tuck her hair into the back of the tunic so that her profile more resembled that of a boy, she allowed him to do so, laughing as he had difficulty in confining it all.

'This is such fun,' he said. 'You are going to be a natural model.'

When she had been sitting for a few minutes he asked, 'Are you finding it uncomfortable?'

'Not at all,' she replied truthfully.

'Good . . . good.' He continued painting, with quick darting movements of the brush, and said quietly as if to himself, 'It's perfect. You can relax, and yet the pose is still alive.'

She did not fully understand his words, but felt proud. His need of her person to complete his picture gave her a sense of importance she had never experienced before.

It was noticing how solid Lizzy's legs look in that particular painting that gave me a key to the scene. Normally she is depicted in long dresses that accentuate her willowy torso, and the few written descriptions there are of her say she was slim. But slender people can have sturdy legs, and as I have always suffered from thick legs myself I imagined how she might have felt after exchanging her long skirt for a pair of tights. Then on the few occasions I have sat for paintings I have been uncomfortable, fidgety, and a damn nuisance to the artists, so it was easy to envisage Lizzy — who both liked modelling and was good at it — behaving in quite the opposite manner.

I realise that this example may seem rather incongruous to readers who want to write science-fiction or spy thrillers, but it is only from one's own work that one can extract with certainty the various promptings and ingredients. I have included it just for that reason — not as an exemplar.

I will not pretend that some publishers are not both cynical and calculating when they plan their category programmes. Although they are, on the whole, fairly respectful of the talent of their top professional writers, much of their output is run-of-the-mill and they treat it as such. If they think there is a rising market in titillating historical romance then they'll commission two or three and refer to them fondly as 'bodice rippers'. If sea yarns are in, they'll trawl for suitable authors. But within this commercialisation there is still room for proper regard on the part of the author for crisp writing, fresh description, original characterisation and well-constructed narrative. As Fielding Gray, the author hero of Simon Raven's series of novels *Alms for Oblivion* says: 'I never said I was an artist. I am an entertainer. I arrange words in pleasing patterns in order to make money. I try to give good value — to see that my patterns are well-wrought — but I do not delude myself by inflating the nature of my function. I try to be neat, intelligent and lucid; let others be "creative" or "inspired".'

I would suggest that the most elusive talent of all in fiction writing is the ability to tell a good story, and it is the one that the genre writer most sorely needs. Almost all readers share John Fowles's 'unlimited greed' for irresistible narrative. And the working out of such a narrative, seeing that your 'patterns are well-wrought', can be fascinating; particularly if you work in a category where extremes and extravagances are permitted.

But it can also be infuriating. Any student who throws down a mediocre suspense story claiming 'I can do better than that', should beware. Once you start to search for an original idea for a murder, or a haunting, or a cosmic disaster, you are embarking on an extremely difficult journey. Finding the original, watertight idea is hard enough in itself; but stretching it out for 200 pages in a manner which will keep your reader on tenterhooks requires skill and energy in exacting amounts. The frustrations of the floppy plot, the plot that never takes on a feeling of compulsion and inevitability, are legion.

I believe that Sir Richard Steele may have been right when he said, 'I have often thought that a story-teller is born, as well as a poet.'

Chapter Nine

Some Other Arts and Entertainments

Before attempting in the next chapter to explore how one learns to look critically at a finished novel, I would like to comment on some of the other arts that absorb people's time. Some regard them as the novelist's competitors. Since I prefer the principle of reciprocity within the theory of evolution to the competitive principle, I regard the other arts as fruitful companions to the novel.

In the average living-room there is a television set, the means to play records, cassettes and radio, and a shelf or table containing books and magazines. Images and music are easily available in a way that was unimaginable a generation ago, and the many forms of words awaiting our attention are bewilderingly diverse. Where among the plays, ballads, political discussions, war reminiscences, operas — soap, grand and light — gossip columns, pop songs, interviews, documentaries, pet-care manuals, politicians' diaries and joke books does the novel find its place?

Not, I would suggest, by haughtily ignoring the rest.

Complaints that television is creating a society which cannot read are commonplace; and yet the bookshops are bursting with new titles. Are they bought for their shiny covers and never opened, or are the complaints really about the fact that millions of people read punchy modern books but not the copious classics?

Yet when one of those classics is adapted for television or the cinema, it is reprinted with a cover photograph of the leading actors and bought by thousands of people who had not given earlier editions a second glance.

What, if anything, can we make of this?

First of all, those who did not grow up with television, and who perhaps still do not regard it very seriously, should not underestimate its capacity to train an alert mind to follow, and expect, the most sophisticated narrative techniques. Fleeting verbal and visual clues, complex allusions, delicate acting — these can occur in all kinds of programmes, sometimes most unexpectedly. It is not by any means always the culturally prestigious programmes which are the best.

Impatient, precocious children learn to turn away from pedestrian adaptations, clumsy dialogue, and dull camerawork, and to seek out what is skilful, versatile, authentic and witty. And with their expectations of narrative entertainment thus heightened, they will look critically at the fiction they read. There will always be some for whom books past, present and future contain few barriers, but for many the literature of the recent past is forbidding.

Take a book that starts like this:

> When Farmer Oak smiled, the corners of his mouth spread till they were within an unimportant distance of his ears, his eyes were reduced to chinks, and diverging wrinkles appeared round them, extending upon his countenance like the rays in a rudimentary sketch of the rising sun.
>
> His Christian name was Gabriel, and on working days he was a young man of sound judgment, easy motions, proper dress, and general good character. On Sundays he was a man of misty views, rather given to postponing, and hampered by his best clothes and umbrella: upon the whole, one who felt himself to occupy morally that vast middle space of Laodicean neutrality which lay between the Communion people of the parish and the drunken section, – that is, he went to church, but yawned privately by the time the congregation reached the Nicene creed, and thought of what there would be for dinner when he meant to be listening to the sermon.

By now, some readers may be yawning too. Yet when *Far from the Madding Crowd*, of which that is the opening, was reprinted to coincide with showings of the film, how did newcomers to Hardy, who had enjoyed the film, find it? Perhaps with the images already implanted in their minds, and the knowledge of the relationships to come, they were able to relax and allow the more discursive parts to hold their attention.

But for others, I would suggest, such writing is off-putting because the descriptive style seems old-fashioned and some of the allusions are unfamiliar. That neither renders Hardy obsolete nor the reader a complete ignoramus; it just reminds us that manners and perceptions change. And what one hopes the film will have done is to lead the new reader to the essence of Hardy where nothing has changed: the inevitable and incalculable effects of love and sex-attraction. Then, once having overcome the barrier of the dated presentation, that reader will have always available to him the fictional panorama of the near past as well as of the present.

Given, however, that many people's natural hunger for stories and entertainment is partially or largely satisfied by visual and spoken narrative — what extra can the modern novel give? What will take a person out of the communal living-room, away to a quiet place, in order to read?

Mainly, I believe, that special feeling of having private access to another person's experience and thoughts.

However good a screen presentation may be, it is a team affair. The team includes an author of course, and in the early stages he probably works on his own. But even then he has the rest of the team at the back of his mind, and later on the producer, director, script editor, cameramen, lighting engineers, soundtrack people, and actors all join in to make their complex and manifold contributions. The result may be magnificent. But while watching it you do not feel you are in private audience with the author. In a film he cannot *say*, straight down the line, what he thinks. In a book, he can. He can also give far more space to his own thoughts and those of his characters. This gives the reader the feeling not so much that he is observing a story, but that he is there, right in it; and of course the images the reader creates in his mind to represent the people and places in the book are his own, constructed from both the information the author gives and his own experience.

'Novels,' wrote Elizabeth Jane Howard, 'are for understanding and finding out about people; language is for making things plain; the more a novelist thinks it is important for the reader to understand exactly what he means, the more trouble he must take to express himself as simply as he can contrive.'

At the beginning of Elizabeth Jane Howard's novel *After Julius* there is this description:

> She woke at exactly quarter past seven in a back bedroom in the top floor of a house in Lansdowne Road. In fourteen minutes the telephone would ring, and a man's voice — charged with that sense of routine emergency that she associated with war films: 'enemy bearing green 320' — would tell her that it was seven-thirty, which of course, she would know already. But when she tried cancelling the telephone, she didn't wake up at all.

The screen could show the girl lying awake, and then receiving the alarm call; could show the girl's tense anticipation. But it could not economically convey the war-film image plus the character point about not waking at all if the call was not booked. It is this quite complex detail that helps to form an intimacy between the author (though the details may not actually be personal to Elizabeth Jane Howard) and any reader who, like the girl, never discovered an easy way to get up on time. And once the intimacy is there, the reader wants to learn more.

The opening of *Far from the Madding Crowd* would have seemed immediate in its time (and of course still does to practised Hardy readers); but language and events change in subtle ways. Even *After Julius,* published in 1965, may already be slightly distanced by events. Television has kept war films familiar, but alarm calls are now so expensive that it would probably not be routine for a young publisher's editor to have one daily, particularly with the advent of efficient digital alarms.

So, while I am not advocating detailed contemporaneity just for its own sake, a writer who is generous with his private insights and original observation of the period we all share, will probably attract a readership.

Kurt Vonnegut Jr, when he conceived *Breakfast of Champions* — which is described as a mixture of 'science fiction, memoir, parable, fairy tale, social comedy and farce' — came up with something that could only be conveyed intimately, writer to reader. Like this.

> Listen: Bunny's mother and my mother were different sorts of human beings, but they were both beautiful in exotic ways, and they both boiled over with chaotic talk about love and peace and wars and evil and desperation, of better days coming by and by, of worse days coming by and by. And both our mothers committed suicide. Bunny's mother ate Drano. My mother ate sleeping pills, which wasn't nearly as horrible.

Convert that to the screen, and you would lose out.

Some novels are the very opposite of intimate; they do not grab your lapels or your sympathy, but are so constructed that the measure of the words demands your full attention. These novels build unfamiliar pictures, and may be set in nameless places, sometimes unaccoutred with identifiable social trappings. The resonances of their words are honed to fill the gaps in one's receiving imagination. But at their best they are not woolly novels. They are strong, and the prose is firm.

J. M. Coetzee is one of these writers. This is from *Waiting for the Barbarians*:

> The children never doubt that the great old tree in whose shade they play will stand forever, that one day they will grow to be strong like their fathers, fertile like their mothers, that they will live and prosper and raise their own children and grow old in the place where they were born. What has made it impossible for us to live in time like fish in water, like birds in the air, like children? It is the fault of Empire! Empire has created the time of history. Empire has located its existence not in the smooth, recurrent spinning time of the cycle of the seasons but in the jagged time of rise and fall, of beginning and end, of catastrophe.

Coetzee has, like his fellow countryman, playwright Athol Fugard, the power to make prose ring. It is a power which can be electric in the theatre, but it succeeds in novels by only a select few. And of those few, it is the ones who unite it with a strong, universal theme, who transcend.

It is not a style for the earnest amateur to attempt.

Many novels do not have unique features that might lure people out of the living-room and away from the entertainment machines. They are novels which are taken up when the entertainment machines are absent — in trains, in beds, at bus stops, in waiting-rooms — or when the machines seem to pall. But what these novels will need is a skill that is equal to the combined skills of the screen teams. There really is no point in writing an entertainment whose characterisation, narrative power and descriptive vividness can be capped by several television or radio programmes daily. The new audience steeped in screen fiction rightly expects a lot from the books it reads.

Writers have long used other art forms as keys or frameworks for novels: operas, myths, symphonies — even paintings. The more open one is to other fields, the more elements one gains for one's own.

I confess to no deep liking either for ballet or for murder stories, and much regret that so few people write books that make me laugh. But with *A Bullet in the Ballet* by Caryl Brahms and S.J. Simon I capitulate still, after nearly thirty years, as soon as I read the first three paragraphs — which contain a murder and a ballet, and do make me laugh.

> Since it is probable that any book flying a bullet in its title is going to produce a corpse sooner or later — here it is.
>
> Dressed somewhat extravagantly in trousers of red and yellow check. Its white jumper is scalloped with scarlet and jade. It wears a yellow bouffon wig, Russian clown's hat and undertaker's gloves. It is bending over the top of a booth, its arms swinging limply over the sides. There is a neat little bullet hole in the centre of its forehead.
>
> It died magnificently in the presence of two thousand people, most of whom had paid for their seats.

If Roy Plomley had invented a *Desert Island Openings*, that would be one of mine. The ballet by the way, for the uninitiated like myself, is *Petroushka*, and the whole book is structured around it.

Owen Brookes quite often finds parallels in music for themes in his writing, and he has given me this example from the novel on which he is now working. Not only does it demonstrate how music may influence a writer, but it also gives an insight into a particular author's method. The book in question, *The Gatherer*, is an occult novel in which the vividness of the setting is of prime importance. The reader must be absorbed by the apparently normal world that the characters inhabit so that when the terrors or mysteries occur he will be both frightened by the events themselves and fearful for the fate of the protagonists.

This is an extract from *The Gatherer*, followed by Owen Brookes's comments:

> A sign announced worm-like bends for the next mile. She changed down a gear as the road began to rise and twist, a serpent between hedged fields that stretched to the glaring horizon. The radio, flipped on out of habit, played something triumphal, unknown, with a blare of brass. The music heightened her mood as she reached up to adjust the sunshade. She seemed to be ascending directly towards the sun. The higher she twisted and climbed, the more evident the snow became. It lay like a frosting on one face of the tilled ridges, turning the fields to a striped pattern of brown-black and white. Stretches of the road ahead were coated with a white carpet through which the incisive tracks of a tractor were clearly marked. Soon she saw that tractor, red-gleaming, way off to the left, cutting deep furrows in the earth. The road ahead was virgin, at least for that day, stressing the isolation of Hemming.
>
> It was not isolation that she felt, however, as the road, after one last, dramatic twist, disgorged her onto the edge of a limitless plain. The hedges ceased, leaving the fields open to the road. A solitary tree, a large and imposing horse-chestnut, stood like a sentinel against the blazing sky. Bright blue now, crystalline as the glaze on exquisite Japanese pottery, but washed over with yellow, with the blaze of the sun. Catching her breath, Sue slowed down, adjusted the sunshade even lower, and stared around her. The fields stretched on either side to a false, dipping horizon. Ahead, beyond the stark tree, she could make out buildings, small and sharp as a child's models. All around her the ribs of snow augmented the light to the garish dazzle of an op-art painting. As though timed, planned to coincide with this rushing moment, the music erupted into a climax, silvery and magisterial. Reaching to turn up the suddenly so fitting sound, she recognised the last trump of Verdi's *Requiem*, gorgeous and terrible.

Owen Brookes writes: 'The above scene was very consciously written but what is interesting about it, from a technical or craft point of view, is the unconscious element in it.

'The landscape, the light, the snow were all very precisely recalled from recent, actual experience, from, in fact, deliberate research. I was "in control" of the material, shaping it to a conscious, desired end. I cannot, still, explain why the car radio, the music, was introduced. It is also uncharacteristic of me to be vague about a piece of music. I tend to place music in my work deliberately and to name it precisely. Yet I wrote, with no idea at all in mind, that it was "unknown" ie to Sue, the character. At that time it was also unknown to me. It was only when I got to the climax of the scene that I realised the blaze of light, the immensity of the landscape could be matched and reinforced by the *Dies Irae* of the Verdi *Requiem.* And so I named the music, invoked it.

'It so happened that, during the period when I was looking at the landscape and preparing to start the book, I was also listening to a tape of the Verdi *Requiem.* The association between the two was obviously deeper than I realised and my subconscious recalled the connection as I was writing.

'That, in itself, is not particularly remarkable. What is is the aptness of the choice, the unplanned resonance citing that piece of music in that context lends to the whole book. Those who read beyond this point discover that the landscape described is primarily the setting for a violent death which will bring Sue great personal grief, will cause her to mourn. The substance of the book is thus foreshadowed in that moment. An idea is planted for those readers who want it.

'The point is, it wasn't planned. It is an example of one of the many "things that just happen" when one is writing well, which lend a piece of writing its sub-text, texture and resonance. It is what makes writing "take off" and what brings the writer satisfaction. Such moments can never be planned, but the author must always be open to them and can, by listening to music (just one example) stock the subconscious like a storehouse which will, as long as one's luck holds, offer up what is needed at the right moment.'

The two arts that are particularly close to me are painting and pop music. This doesn't mean I prefer pop to classical, or painting to drama, but I have what I can only describe as a more personal relationship with them. They frequently fuel my imagination, and the imagination of some of my characters. The following is an example that concerns a painting. It is taken from my novel *A Pillar of Cloud* which is about two strangers, both married, who meet and have a love affair. Here they are visiting a small municipal art gallery. Colin is the woman's husband.

> 'That's a painting Colin would like,' she said.
>
> He looked at an image on white paper of two rectangles, delineated by, and bespattered with, myriads of different coloured

sprayed spots of paint. In some areas the spots gathered in a dense crowd, in others they were scattered like distant people fleeing indiscriminately from a disaster. The colours combined to give an overall impression of indigo and aquamarine.

'Why?'

'Because it combines classical and romantic. Because it's non-assertive, yet sure. And because it respects geometry, painting, and science.'

He looked at it again. 'Do you like it?'

'Very much indeed.'

He realised that her bonds with Colin were of a different nature to her bonds with him. The painting was one which he would have passed without a second glance, yet into it she could read a whole credo for Colin. He wondered which picture she would have selected to appeal particularly to him, but he did not ask her. He was beginning to realise the fruitlessness of creating such links between them, of encouraging her imagination to reach out yet further towards his. He looked once more at the spots and rectangles. Colin was beginning to impinge on him as a real person, as his rival for Alison's attention. Colin could find sense and feeling in something which he did not understand at all. Was he then ignorant, or the boy who sussed out the emperor?

For the curious, the painting is a small one by Ian Stephenson.

A particular way in which I find painting informs the imagination is by fixing landscapes. Camus said, 'But landscapes slip away and are forgotten. This is why there are painters.' I don't mean by this that instead of describing a Suffolk landscape you describe a particular Constable. But familiarity with Constable may help you to look at Suffolk with a more informed eye. Close observations of landscape and weather, which have to be written down as soon as possible — one seldom retains them for long with complete accuracy — are useful to particularise the painterly focus. Here is a Northamptonshire one from my folder:

Blue November day; the noon sun low and dazzling; blurs of fog still dispersing in patches; a bare tall ash in the hedgerow, its top branches still coated with frost, white against a Mediterranean sky. The frost dripping in the sun, from that tree and the copse across the road, the only noise apart from birdsong.

This is not an exciting description in itself, but it enables me to recall exactly how the scene looked to me, and how it made me feel, well over a year later.

David Fletcher, one of the main characters in my second novel *A Fleshly School* (and its sequels *Linsey-Woolsey* and *Paradise*), shares my love of the poetry of Gerard Manley Hopkins, and in one scene this coalesces with the potent effect of pop music. A pop band is performing at a dance in the art school where David, who is drunk, works.

> Every now and then the groups of jerking dancers erupted to the violent climaxes and sudden cliff-hanging breaks in the rhythm, but focus remained on the singer.
>
> An imitation of a record, played a thousand times in his memory, severed all constraints. I am falling dying. *Dangerous; does set danc-ing blood — the O-seal-that-so-feature.* To watch, and listen. *Self flashes off frame and face.* That book, that tattered book, torn between them, the helpless pristine springness of the pink and green cover (an artist's idea of a harmless starlit apple-blossom impression?) grubby for ever. *To what serves mortal beauty*?
>
> He tried to focus. Drew himself up on a window ledge; concentrated. At the end of each verse the leader went into a pleasing caterwaul, tilting back his pretty head and spidering his arms and legs.
>
> *How meet beauty*? *Merely meet it.* The performance continued, heightened — drawing its essential fertilisation from the shouting, intermittently screaming, weaving students. His voice was like sandpaper burnt by sad knowledge. *Then leave, let that alone.*
>
> No. The tincted hair which the singer shook away each, frequent, time it fell forward, married with Elinor's elusive, shaking mantle. When at the end he froze in the centre of the stage, his head flopping forward, David was on to the stage, had walked straight up to him, and kissed the already retreating bony cheek.

The words in italics are from Hopkins's *To What serves Mortal Beauty*? and the pink and green cover is the one that used to adorn the Penguin edition of his selected writings in the Sixties.

Twelve years after I completed the first draft of *A Fleshly School*, I began to write a biography of Hopkins and I had by then quite forgotten about his inclusion in that novel. Even when I wrote about sprung rhythm in these terms, I did not remember it.

> . . . that intuition was the over-riding source of his poetry is surely true, and it is one of the reasons why he has remained so popular with a particular audience.
>
> That audience is one which does not mind having its nerve-ends played on; that enjoys the delicate stop and start, crest-of-the-wave rise and packed syntactical descent of Hopkins's unpredictable lines. His rhythms, if they are reminiscent of anything, are similar to those of imaginative sexual touch; not the

regular pounding of beat that can make sex, music, poetry or field-work dull, but the inventive cross-rhythms and suspense that may be found in lovemaking, in Beethoven and ragtime, in street rhymes, and in black work-songs where the beat hangs in temporary limbo over the rest bars. (W. H. Gardner wrote that 'Sprung rhythm is, in effect, a syncopated rhythm, and stands in the same relation to the regular syllabic metres as the prevalent syncopation of modern dance music stands to the regular musical rhythm.')

It was only when I was looking through my early novels for an extract to include in a reading that I rediscovered David's interest in Hopkins and realised I had foreshadowed that description a decade earlier.

My son Dan, who was a baby in Chapter 2 of this book, grew up to be a musician and songwriter. After thirty years of listening to pop, I was privileged to hear at first hand what it is like to spend days in the recording studio with producers and engineers, separating out the instrumental tracks and the vocals, criticising and polishing each element until the final mix is at last achieved, and all the time not losing sight of the songs that Dan and his partner Barb built up from a bar of melody, or a line of lyric, or a particular rhythm, or a feeling, flake by flake — like the writer echoing the sculptor. Familiarity with this process helped him when recently he changed tack and wrote his first novel.

It is both enriching and reassuring to have insights into a creative process other than your own. The end products may appear worlds apart, but some of the stations along the journey often seem very familiar.

Recently I was listening to Trevor Nunn being interviewed on the radio about the Royal Shakespeare Company's successful stage adaptation of Dickens's novel *Nicholas Nickleby*. It lasts for over eight hours, and the company intended it as a short-lived experiment, never dreaming that the public would flock to see it. They wanted, Nunn explained, to see if they could recreate via the stage that sense of 'losing oneself' in a book. They succeeded. And demonstrated that by being open to the particular magic of another art form, they were able to enrich their own.

Chapter Ten

How Can I Improve My Novel?

You've taken all the help you can from other people, or you don't wish to show your work to anyone yet. You've been told, or sense, that the book is not yet 'right'. And you have a feeling of responsibility towards it — it still interests you enough for you to want to make improvements. It has something going for it, and deserves further diligence. How can you alter the marks on this floppy pack of pages so that they take on a firmer character and become less easy to put down? How do you get to the stage where you feel in some measure to be in control?

First, I think, put the manuscript away for at least a month, preferably longer, and try to forget about it. During that period read other people's books, watch plays, listen to poetry — what ever takes your fancy; but allow your mind to experience freely other people's creations.

Then set aside a quiet time when you can read your manuscript through and make comments and assessments. Perhaps a weekend, or the consecutive evenings of a single week. But an intense period so that you have a chance to view your book as a whole.

It may be that you will end up wanting to reject it entirely. As long as this is a sense of having passed through a stage, of no longer having the interest to improve the structure and the texture of the writing because you genuinely feel the theme is not important enough, that is fine. It is particularly fine if you already have a new theme bubbling up which you are excited about. But please don't reject the book on the grounds that you have failed because it is not as good as the Ruth Rendell or the Malcolm Bradbury or the John Updike you have been reading, even though you feel it is still valid as an idea. Most writers' first efforts never see the light of day. Learning to improve is the hardest part of all.

If, however, after careful thought, you know in your heart of hearts you would rather stop altogether now in case you never improve enough to satisfy your own standards, if you sense you are a lover of literature but feel rather tetchy and tepid about the assumption of authorship, then perhaps you should heed what Gide used to say to young writers who wrote asking him if they should carry on: 'What? You can stop yourself writing and you hesitate?'

But, for the others . . .

However blindly you may have begun the book, and with however close a vision you may have stumbled through it (with my full encouragement), at this stage you should try to assume a measure of control.

Theme and plot

What I hope that reading the manuscript through after a break will do first of all is to reveal weaknesses in theme and plot.

Do you now have a clear overall idea what the book is about, and can you see the main mechanisms of the story? (Some of you, of course, will have been able to do this all along. Though you may be surprised when you come to take a detached overview how your aim has to an extent become muddied, or your plot has some flimsy hinges.)

Let us take theme first. Do you believe that your theme is valid and strong? It does not have to be original – people will write about love, revenge, jealousy, ambition and loss until the world ends – but are you *adding* to the theme?

Suppose you are writing about a woman who has two small children and is determined to return to her career, which happens to be architecture. That is your theme: the importance to that character – and perhaps by implication to man in general – of a balance between family love plus private responsibility, and creative fulfilment plus public achievement. It is a theme which has filled many magazine pages and newspaper columns, and has supplied the furniture for several novels. Are you able, through the flesh of your characters' emotions and particularity, to express the theme freshly and to tell a narrative that will draw the reader into caring about your protagonists? There should not be pages of exposition where you, the author, explain in a pedestrian way how the problems of conflicting responsibility affect your characters. We should see the conflict through their eyes – their action and their thoughts. And although obviously the novel can contain only what you have experienced, observed and can imagine, by allowing your various characters to develop the theme you will probably find you can imagine more than you realised. Rather than imposing merely the views developed during your particular life, you can give those views (or some of them) to one person, and allow another – whose background and reasoning you must be able to envisage even though you don't share the former or agree with the latter – to express different ones. And from that a plot will naturally occur, and the theme thus develop.

Try to put yourself in the position of the reader. Can you honestly expect him to feel involved with your characters (do *you* get caught up by the power of the writing when you re-read after a gap?) and are the developments in the plot convincing and either exciting or interesting enough to drive him on to the end of the book?

If the answer to the latter part of the question is 'no', then summarise the plot development points on one sheet of paper and look at them hard. How could you make them more dramatic? Have you exploited fully the situations the psychology of your characters will create and the results that their actions will cause? Don't cure a weak plot by piling on complications, especially not by adding a host of minor characters, but by getting full value out of what is already there.

If you have a murderer escaping from the police, rather than arrange a convenient but unconvincing road accident to hold him up, perhaps set that scene in bad weather which will affect both the murderer and the police — and you can choose exactly how and when each party will be affected. A natural, inescapable phenomenon such as weather is often much more believable than a hasty intervention from outside, but you will need strong descriptive powers to convey the fright and frustration of a desperate man driving through fog/snow/gale together with the determination and anger of the people chasing him.

Returning to the case of the woman architect who wishes to resume her career. Have you had several separate scenes between her and, say, her husband, her best friend, her nosy neighbour, her mother, but barely attempted to bring three of these characters together or, perhaps, to have a scene between the husband and the mother without the architect? By not always relying on your central character to fuel the development, you get variety and choice from the possibilities that the interaction of other people, other psychologies, will cause. I mentioned that she had two children. Have they been allowed proper character space, and not been reduced to tweeness or sub-identity? Even if she doesn't see them very clearly, her best friend might.

If, on the other hand, the book is deliberately anchored in its central character, perhaps told in the first person, then have you told us enough to make it really interesting; dug deep enough to make us care about the theme as she experiences it? Often, as Orwell said about Joyce 'It is a matter of *daring* . . . to expose the imbecilities of the inner mind'. You may want to quell those imbecilities, but they could be exactly the original, honest kind of observation that will grab your reader's attention and make him grasp the significance of your theme.

Time and content

Drastic alterations may seem nerve-racking to embark on, but they can have unexpectedly good results. Try not to regard your draft as 'set', open only to minor tinkerings and prunings and additions. Sometimes major surgery works wonders — especially amputation!

Particular portions of time, and the actions which fill that time, are not always indispensable. To delete a four-paragraph morning, with its breakfast, letters, shopping and headache, might be the making of a particular chapter. Or it might sharpen the interest if the order of two chapters, which cover the same time-span told from different characters' viewpoints, are transposed. Such deletions and transpositions usually necessitate small alterations elsewhere, and that in itself can sometimes tighten the writing and the construction.

Assuming control over time, and time's contents, is something the writer does mainly by intuition. Once one starts to look at it too objectively one can get giddy — but occasionally that is beneficial.

Some beginners manage to complete their first novels simply by putting down every minor detail they can think of connected with actions that take place over, say, a week. They have not produced a taut plot, or interesting characters, but just reported a stream of events and descriptions. By reproducing the prosaic contents of those seven days as they pop up in their limited imaginations they have managed to fill 300 pages. They have been taken over by continuous time and insignificant content.

Others, more self-conscious, find it difficult to move through time. They feel it is cheating if, say, they have left their hero clocking-in for the first time at the factory on Monday, and then begin the following chapter thus: 'By Friday morning at eight o'clock, Leonard no longer questioned the procedure, no longer noticed the beer-puffed faces of his fellows, or the smell of the chemicals; his actions had become mechanical and his thoughts hummed around the probable size of the paypacket he would receive at the end of the afternoon like bees humming around a sunflower.' They feel some moral obligation to account for Tuesday, Wednesday and Thursday. But it is only cheating if they have no sense themselves of what happened to Leonard during those three days. As long as they are aware of the changes that have taken place, and are not just positing a change purely for the convenience of the plot, then they should carry their readers along.

Another difficulty some writers encounter is the movement of their characters in space. I don't mean the science-fiction sort of space, but simply getting them in and out of rooms, or from Leicester to Newcastle. Here again there is no need to describe the movement unless it is significant. It is only when you have a feeble hold on what is happening, and therefore dread that your reader will mistrust you, that you need to follow your characters' every footstep. Let them disappear and reappear without unnecessary fuss.

The same applies to all content. Only include a scene or a description if it adds something. If you can delete it, and then on reading the passage through two days later not regret its omission, it was superfluous. But if you miss it, feel it was a proper piece of the jig-saw — put it back. Perhaps it just needed a little re-shaping.

Sometimes a section may be necessary to the development of the book, but sit awkwardly, dully, on the page. This may be because you have not the benefit of direct experience or observation to make it come alive. Don't be defeated. Take a can of beer, or a packet of toffees, or a panatella to your desk and just let your imagination open out into the action. Don't rely on what you have read elsewhere. Think, imagine, fantasise — write freely.

You might end up with rubbish. But perhaps you find there is an improvement.

Character

People. How are you to present your people so that they assume an individuality without writing down a complete inventory of their qualities and histories?

Don't make the mistake of thinking physical description is all-important. To be told that a man has brown hair, blue eyes and a fair complexion, gets the reader virtually nowhere. But the last sentence in the following extract from a description of a minor character in Russell Hoban's *Turtle Diary* creates an image you may remember for the rest of your life:

> . . . I think he lives off old ladies. I've no reason to think it except his looks. His eyes look as if he's pawned his real ones and is wearing paste.

There is nothing wrong with straightforward physical description, but you must 'see' your character, like a painter looking at his sitter, and not just reach for the kind of information included on a police 'Wanted' poster. In his story *The Cloud*, which is told in a deliberately painterly manner, John Fowles says of a character:

> Bel is thirty-one, four years older than her sister, a prettier

woman, plumper and rounder-faced, pale face and fox red hair, more Irish, dry grey-green Irish eyes, though the blood is only from a grandmother's side and they have never lived there, lack the accent. In her old straw-hat and her loose-sleeved cream dress she looks a little of the matron, the eccentric, the latterday lady of letters; always in shadow, her freckled skin is allergic to the sun.

You can now 'see' Bel, would be able to pick her out in a crowd of strangers. An artist could make a drawing of her.

It is perfectly possible, however, to write a whole book about someone without ever revealing the colour of their hair or the shape of their face. The reader may not even notice that these details are not mentioned, for if you have made the character seem real through your description of his actions and thoughts, and by the words he speaks, the reader will quickly make his own visual images.

There can be a danger in 'fixing' a character too exactly — like a butterfly on a pin, or a bee in aspic. It is all right for a minor character, whose personality does not undergo any change during the book and whose role is to act precisely within their character, but for a leading character you need to leave room for growth or change.

In *Aspects of the Novel,* E.M. Forster describes these two types of character as 'flat and round'. The 'flat' ones, he says, have the advantage of being 'easily recognized whenever they come in,' and 'are very useful to the author, since they never need reintroducing, never run away, have not to be watched for development, and provide their own atmosphere — little luminous disks of pre-arranged size, pushed hither and thither like counters across the void . . .' Dickens excels at these; so does Angus Wilson. 'The test of a round character,' Forster continues, 'is whether it is capable of surprising in a convincing way. If it never surprises, it is flat.'

That last statement, like so many of Forster's, is deceptively simple. I think it provides a key to why some books are so intriguing, and others just so-so. In real life, we tend to tire of our friends' problems when they seem endlessly repetitive, giving us a vision of a particular syndrome continuing with no respite or change until death. It makes us feel impotent. But when a friend bravely (or even blindly) endeavours to alter the apparently irrevocable course, not only our sympathy but also our interest is aroused. For the ability to change is what gets a person out of the aspic and away from the butterfly pin, and into the realm where choice and creativity exist. And one of the chief causes of change in a character in a novel is the effect and influence that other characters have upon him.

One hears of novelists being 'carried away' by their characters — a phenomenon I have not experienced. It is more like sharing part of one's life with them, and it is true that they sometimes take a course of action one had not previously planned. Occasionally that can produce the Forsterian effect of 'surprising in a convincing way'. Your involvement with your main characters needs to be close enough to allow their emotions and actions to develop in a manner that makes them sufficiently interesting and unique to command the reader's concern. When you read through your manuscript, try to look dispassionately at your characters and discover whether you have managed to present them so that the reader will care about their predicament. Have you conveyed the intensity and the individuality of their situation which was what made you want to write about them in the first place?

Dialogue

Some students find dialogue easy. The danger then is that they may allow their characters to witter on quite realistically but to no particular point. Some find it difficult to speak in any voice other than their own. Some tend to use dialogue as a vehicle for thought and make their characters speak in an unconvincing, stiff sort of way. Some, to begin with, find it almost impossible to get their characters to open their mouths and speak at all.

For me, probably the most intuitive part of writing is the switching between speech and description. Apart from sometimes deleting short passages of boring interchange, I hardly ever transpose description to speech, or vice versa, when re-writing. Quite a lot of this is to do with the rhythm of the narrative. Dialogue usually speeds things up, description slows it down. It is a kind of change of gear that becomes automatic with practice. And, above all, dialogue is so economical for moving things on — and for depositing little concealed time-bombs into the plot. (We are all familiar with the situation of suddenly being able to read significance into something that was said to us a while back because of events that have occurred subsequently.) Oddly enough, this does not always need to be calculated. If your characters are developing properly — truthfully — it is possible to read through what you have written the day before and find you have deposited one of these little bombs quite intuitively. Indeed, speech is, I would suggest, usually the most instinctive part of a novel. You are placing yourself in the mouth of anyone from a duke to a dalek, and must make yourself available to reproduce their words.

Some people find it useful to eavesdrop on buses, in restaurants, theatre queues, public lavatories, and jot down overheard snatches of dialogue. If one is not a natural mimic, this helps to increase one's repertoire. Care is needed, for the limited dialogue writer, not to introduce characters who would need to speak at some length with American, Nigerian, Geordie or Belfast voices — none of which the writer can 'hear'. There are ways round this. One can deliberately try to work up a voice, making oneself listen intensely to a particular accent or dialect, or get someone qualified to vet the dialogue you have put into the mouth of, say, an American or a Pakistani.

The best way to test dialogue is to read it aloud. Is it easy to speak? Are they the words which you feel your characters really *would* say? If not, try to think yourself into their parts and see how their speech might be altered to make it more natural. But, as I said earlier, don't let them just chatter on about inanities merely because you've discovered how to make them sound lifelike. (Unless, of course, those inanities are an integral part of the picture you are trying to present.) Their remarks should help to establish their characters, or their relationships with one another, or further the action — or possibly do all three at once.

If appropriate, dialogue is useful for introducing some humour. Being consistently funny is a scarce talent, and no writer should lurch heavy-handedly after laughs. But it is a rare novel that doesn't benefit from a little humour, and as Henry Green said, 'Laughter relaxes the characters in a novel. And if you *can* make the reader laugh he is apt to get careless and go on reading.'

How necessary is it to vary 'he said/she said' and have your characters replying, asking, responding, affirming, whispering, gabbling, shouting, crying, croaking, drawling, droning, stuttering and interrupting? Not *too* necessary. Go lightly. Remember, if there are only two people talking to one another, you don't need to specify the speaker each time. (Though beware having long passages of undifferentiated dialogue that force the reader to count back to the first 'Ann said/John said' in order to find out who is speaking.) To use 'said' all the time becomes dull, but even worse is to have characters who continually bark or spout or ejaculate but seldom simply speak. If there is good reason to use a descriptive verb such as 'shout' or 'gasp' or 'murmur', then by all means do so, but don't over-employ them so that they lose their value.

Description

This covers everything from the pedestrian nuts and bolts of getting Character A down the stairs and out of the house in order to avoid meeting Character B whom he has seen walking up the back garden, to a panoramic evocation of a fishing fleet coming into harbour at dawn.

The most obvious advice is that the style should fit the occasion. There is nothing wrong with someone simply running down the stairs and leaving the house. They don't have to be running quickly (running implies speed), or to slip on the stairs, or to have a tussle with the door knob, but if the appearance of Character B has completely changed Character A's situation, (if, for example, he had thought B was dead), then his exit from the house needs a full description so that the reader can share his feelings.

The fishing fleet at dawn is one of those set pieces that invite heightened prose of the type called purple. You need the eye and ear of a poet to do it well – but it can be worked at; Plante's paragraphs are a good training ground. And of course original heightened description needn't be purple at all – it can be 'cool' or 'spare'. The Fairfax and Moat *The Way to Write* examines the types of image that contribute to descriptive writing, and explores the territory that prose and poetry share.

It is tone of voice plus rhythm and pace that so often govern the success or otherwise of descriptive writing. As with dialogue, try reading a paragraph aloud to see whether it 'falls' right. Be flexible with punctuation. Remember there are such things as semi-colons as well as commas and full-stops. Look at your punctuation as though you were an actor or a musician studying a speech or a sonata that you had to perform. Roughly: a comma equals one rest-beat, a semi-colon or colon two, and a full-stop three.

There are some writers (and many readers) who find pictorial description of the fishing-fleet kind boring. They want to stick close to the characters and the action. No reason why not, just as long as the omission of heightened writing does not mean the omission of all carefully-honed sentences in favour of a kind of second-hand action-prose that has no flavour or individuality.

Grafted-on bits of description, that are stuck there because the writer feels he 'ought' to do some picture-making, usually beg for deletion. The picture should absorb the reader; draw him in – give the sight and sound and smell of the place. Images should be used sparingly. Not all water needs to shimmer like silk (in fact no water needs to). But when you want to draw particular attention to something, to focus your reader's eye or interest slightly more sharply than the actual event apparently warrants, then to create an image that falls naturally on the page and does not seem too deliberate, is most satisfying.

I particularly like the image of the British Museum in the final sentence of this paragraph from *Maurice* by E. M. Forster. However I know, also, that many readers would find the personal tone in the first sentence, the use of 'in its old fashion', fussy. But it is the combination of the intimate with the grand, the leaking roofs with the huge tomb, that pleases me.

> The rain was coming down in its old fashion, tapping on a million roofs and occasionally effecting an entry. It beat down the smoke, and caused the fumes of petrol and the smell of wet clothes to linger mixed on the streets of London. In the great forecourt of the Museum it could fall uninterruptedly, plumb onto the draggled doves and the helmets of the police. So dark was the afternoon that some of the lights had been turned on inside, and the great building suggested a tomb, miraculously illuminated by spirits of the dead.

A versatile imagination, a versatility in one's private thinking rather than always letting the mind wander along well-beaten tracks, develops with practice and a little courage. It makes the time a writer spends at his desk, or indeed moving through the world at large, much more exciting and less liable to stasis. 'Versatility' is not the same as 'richness'. I think it would be difficult to develop a fecund imagination in a normally matter-of-fact person. But the matter-of-fact person can make links, can see 'real' things from different points of view.

The Flashback

This is really part of both 'Plot' and 'Time', but it calls for separate attention. The word was actually coined in 1918 to describe 'the recapitulation of an earlier scene' in a film, and was soon also used to describe 'a revival of the memory of past events in a pictorial or written presentation'. Writers had, of course, been using flashbacks for years, but the cinema dramatised their effect and psychology emphasised their significance.

They are a great boon to the writer, but if over-used can become a great bore to the reader. They can also be badly employed to rescue the writer from an awkward plot. However as a way of deepening the texture of a novel, of revealing the layered strands of time and circumstances that contribute to a person's life, they are sometimes indispensable, and with their help the writer acquires the freedom (and the complications) of the time-traveller.

Check, when you read through your manuscript, to see if you have used them at all; and, if so, whether you consider you have used them well. Do they sit firmly in the narrative, occurring with apparent smoothness, or are they perhaps jerked on rather self-consciously? Would they become less obtrusive if you employed them more frequently, developing a kind of rhythm or patterning in their usage?

If you find you have not included any flashbacks at all, and if one of the criticisms of your work is that it is too flat, lacking real body in the presentation of your characters, then consider whether they might add something. (This is a dangerous suggestion, it sounds rather like cheap cosmetic surgery. But at least by experimenting with flashbacks, using them for the first time, you will learn something.)

The expression of the effects of the past within the present, not just as self-contained flashes of memory but as a continuing influence, have absorbed great twentieth-century novelists such as Marcel Proust and James Joyce, and influenced many lesser ones. But it is difficult, when one sets out on a maiden novel, to grasp the complexities that access to time present and time past can compound; and the skill to use this access usually develops slowly.

It becomes, however, both comforting and challenging to realise that you have not only the present lives of your characters in your hands, but all their past lives too, and then to discover ways of moving confidently between the two.

The Whole

> In all the arts the great problem of the artist is to preserve the force of his intuition, his germ, what is sometimes called his inspiration, throughout the long process of technical construction.
>
> Joyce Cary
>
> The most essential gift for a good writer is a built-in, shock-proof, shit detector.
>
> Ernest Hemingway

I feel I should apologise to those readers who don't like Hemingway's bluntness, but it would not be a very sincere apology. Criticism of one's own writing is a tough business. At first it can be painful, embarrassing and bewildering. Later, when you are able to delude yourself you've written well because you have learned a spontaneous surface competence, it is exasperating to have to admit you've actually produced a whole chapter — or even a whole book — that is null and void.

But if you are to develop as a writer, the ability to write a story down has to be accompanied by an ability to criticise it. The only way to communicate your germ, your intuition, is to gain an understanding of every facet of the edifice which contains it.

Chapter Eleven

Amateur and Professional

It is unfortunate that the word 'amateur' when applied to writers is more often than not used in a derogatory way, and I would like to make a plea for the importance of a particular kind of amateur writer.

These writers have no pressing ambition to be published, but possess a will to write and a need to record and preserve the flavour of their lives and imaginings. Probably their writings will take the form of journals or reminiscences, but sometimes they are presented as fiction – the writer intuitively discovering the freedom gained thereby.

The value of such writing (apart from the satisfaction it gives its author) is, I believe, immeasurable. No home-movie, nor tape recording of a family gathering, can preserve the part of a person that he or she will put into their private writing. To a young person concerned to discover more than just the surface facts of their background, a box of fictions, written by a grandmother or an uncle, might prove a treasure trove. To have access to the imaginations of one's forebears, as well as to their portraits and legal papers, would be fascinating.

But if such writers are to leave behind vivid records, not just docile meanderings, they need to respect the craft of writing; to learn, along with the would-be professional, how to improve. It has long been accepted that people learn to act or sing or draw or dance for their own amusement. I believe they should be encouraged to write narratives too.

One student of eighty-one who read the Fairfax and Moat *The Way to Write*, was prompted by a suggestion in it to write an impression of the funeral of one of her class-mates which took place over seventy years ago. These are three separate extracts from her piece:

> We stood in a thin line at the edge of the pavement, feet close together, arms straight down by our sides, heads slightly bowed.

We, the girl section of 'Standard 2' from the village school. Like Rosie, we were all in our eighth year, and now we stood silently paying homage to Rosie.

Miss Hallam struck her tuning fork, gave us the key.

'Abide with me, fast falls the eventide.'

The sunshine shafted through the tall classroom windows. I wished we could sing 'Summer suns are glowing' for Rosie's sake. I wished we were free of school and Rosie would be racing with us to the 'Recky' to play our favourite games of the moment before tea time. How far, far away had Rosie gone?

A severe winter *could* snatch a small brother or sister away from one of the many small dwellings, overfull with brothers and sisters. But now it was summer time, everywhere bathed in sunlight, and Rosie was an only one.

It was almost as though Rosie's mother was waiting as two or perhaps three of us would pass her kitchen window. She would beckon and ask, would we like a slice of seed cake, or a portion of sponge-cake trifle. But whatever it was she would add "Our Rosie's favourite. Our Rosie in the churchyard." There was pride as well as sadness in her voice as her eyes looked steadfastly through the window in the direction of the churchyard.

One could imagine this writer embarking on something where fact and fiction flowed together into a long narrative, preserving an essence which would otherwise be lost.

And from the other end of the age spectrum, here is part of a short novel which a thirteen-year-old girl wrote during the two terms I had a writer's fellowship at a comprehensive school. She used to come to my room during break, twice a week, and dive into her story with the energy and alacrity of a young dolphin diving into the sea. I hope the writer's children – and grandchildren – will have access to the story of the splendidly laconic Annie Wright.

I woke up and found I still had my clothes on. It was already ten o'clock, which meant another day off work. I got up and went into my brothers' room. No one was there; they must have gone to work.

I changed my crumpled clothes and decided to go shopping, but then I couldn't be bothered. Thomas had said he would go. So I got out my book and lay on my bed reading.

None of us really like reading, but sometimes it is a very good pastime.

'Brr . . . Brr . . .' I could hear the phone ringing in my ears. I got up.

'Hello. Miss Wright here.'

'Oh Annie. Thank God you're in.'

'Who is it?'
'Don't you know? Peter!'
'Oh, sorry Pete.'
'That's all right. Look, I must see you. It's important.'
'Oh no! What?'
'Look, can I come round?'
'OK. When?'
'I'll make for the flat right now.'
'OK.' and I put the phone down. Peter is my boyfriend.
He claims that he loves me. Hah! He's going to Australia soon. Something to do with his job he tells me. I've known him for years, since school. There was a knock on the door and I let Peter in.
'Oh hello,' I said.
'Hello darling.'
'What's up?' I said, wanting to get straight to the point.
'Make us a cup of coffee, and I'll tell you.'
'OK. then.' I went to the kitchen cupboard, but all I could find was the tin of green beans and the stale bread. On the sideboard were five bottles of milk.
'You'll have to make do with milk.'
'OK. then.'
'Hot or cold?'
'I don't mind.'
'One or the other!'
'Make it water.'
'OK.' So we sat down on the floor with a mug of water each. (We have broken all our glasses.)
'Well, what is it?'
'My trip to Australia. I've got to go early next Friday.'
I felt disappointed. I thought he was going to tell me something really important, but I suppose it was important to him so I tried to look sad. I could not think of anything to say. (Nor could he.)
'Um . . . I . . . sorry . . . sorry . . .'
'Will you come with me?' he bleated out.
That was the last thing I wanted to do. Fancy going to another country where nobody knew you except for one boring boy like Peter. I suppose it seems as if I don't like him. Well I do — in a strange way.
'Well will you?'
'Peter, you are very kind and honest to me, but you must understand that I can't . . . well, let me put it this way . . .'
'You don't love me, that's it!'
That was exactly it.

Other amateur writers will not be content to write for themselves and their families and friends, but will continue to submit their work to publishers. They should try to be critically honest, and not waste postage on very sub-standard work; should avoid the trap I have already mentioned of attending a writers' circle whose members are far too lenient (or uninformed) in their judgements; and should perhaps widen their reading. If one's own work is beginning to pall, English Literature evening classes might provide a tonic. Don't become too disgruntled while trying to seek success and garnering only rejection slips. If you value the words you put on paper, it is worth regularly giving some of your time to improving and adding to them. Apart from anything else, fashions change, and something which is unwanted now might acquire an unexpected import in a decade's time. However, if what you are trying to do is to be a commercial success because it looks easy and you don't think much of many of the writers who are published — well, I have indicated earlier in this book what I feel about that attitude.

One of the disadvantages of being an amateur novelist is that, unlike the amateur poet, there is no relatively cheap and simple way that you can reproduce your work for limited circulation. And the little presses and community publishing ventures can seldom afford to print full-length novels either. However a few of the latter — Centerprise in London is a notable example — do tackle novels that have a specific interest for the community. To become involved in such a project, whether or not it leads to publication of your own work, can be very rewarding. Your Regional Arts Association should know whether there are any community or co-operative publishing ventures in your area.

Whatever happens, don't get involved with what is known as Vanity Publishing. This means paying for your novel to be printed by a firm which will probably claim that they will publish and distribute it, but in fact do nothing of the sort. You are left with a very large bill and bulky packages of books which you will not be able to sell.

Because writing is such a private activity, some authors shrink from displaying their wares under any amateur or community umbrella, wanting their manuscripts to go straight from their desk to an unknown publisher's reader while remaining completely invisible themselves. Very, very understandable. But if none of the publishers come up trumps, then the writer is left without any audience at all — a situation few performers can sustain for ever.

You can only choose to give up or stick it out — or overcome your shyness and experiment with meeting other writers.

David Storey had written six or seven novels before he had *This*

Sporting Life accepted for publication. Then he wrote *Flight Into Camden* 'in eighteen days in a flush of enthusiasm at the acceptance'.

You could say he became a professional only after this first success. But it is a sign of the professional that he or she is prepared to write six or seven novels without achieving any success.

Chapter Twelve

A Postscript Prompted by Mr Cary Grant's Insomnia

Cary Grant was reported to have said, 'I usually wake around three and read for an hour or so. Never fiction. If it's not true, what's the point of it?'

You'll find there are quite a lot of people who agree with him. Facts, verifiable facts, are what they believe will enable them to get to grips with the world. To read a novel is to fritter away time. Stories are for kids and idle women — and they'd be better off without them: *The Tale of Little Red Riding Hood* only makes children nervous of their grandmothers, and George Eliot gave women strange ideas. People's lives — they're interesting. But only when they're true. Biographies, autobiographies. Imaginative lives? What *is* the point?

They do not understand that the process of making good fiction is a journey into truth. That by convincing and involving a reader in your theme, your setting, your characters, you have given him something to add to the knowledge we all collect which helps us to understand more about other people and about ourselves.

Could anyone really believe that *Anna Karenina* tells you nothing about love and infidelity and rejection and despair that could not be better learned from a journalist's factual reconstruction of the events leading to a woman's suicide?

But it has to be admitted that some share Mr Grant's view because they have read mainly bad novels. Or novels that do not appeal to them. They have not discovered the fiction writers who would enthral them. Perhaps they put up too much of a resistance. Perhaps they will not admit that the way characters in novels ponder and agonise, get into tangles, allow themselves to be deceived and enraptured, is 'real life'. For they deny the speculative, vulnerable parts of themselves. They are well organised. They do not dream — or else they ignore the content of their dreams. Which may be why some of them suffer from insomnia.

By writing this book, I may encourage the production of some bad novels. But it worries me more that by now I might have discouraged a potentially good writer; that my words, my tone, might have caused even one sensitive person to walk away from an art they had thought they might practise. In that case I wish they could forget everything I have written, and just concentrate on proving to all the Cary Grants that there *is* a point to fiction.

Writing, said Doris Lessing, is 'like digging in a huge pile of sand with a very small spade.'

Anyone who has benefited from reading a body of her work will know that Doris Lessing has attempted to come to grips with the meaning of her own pile more comprehensively than almost any other living writer. We all have a pile of sand to work from, but not all of us can see the extent of it. We tend instead to see just the surface, and are not prepared to use our small spade, our mind, to discover the depths.

In some ways it *is* easier for writers who have experience of events of obvious universal interest to know where to begin. Doris Lessing's African roots and politicisation are crucial — but she takes her spade to reveal the individual not to shape portentous theories. And there is a need for writers of all backgrounds to take their situation seriously. The unpredictable forces that change societies are gathering speed. No factual information-processor can keep up with them. The novelist makes leaps in the imaginative dark. He wants to understand.

Since publishers do not want serious novels that are also formless and dull, (and I am afraid in these panicky, recessive times quite often don't want shapely, interesting ones either), the writer who is willing to tackle the fundamental issues of his society and hopes to reach a wide audience has got to be very very good indeed.

It is worth encouraging the art of fiction writing among thousands to throw up one enduring novel. That novel may not come from an obvious 'genius'. Hard work and a belief in sticking at it against the odds could produce an important book thirty years hence from a writer who is now young and writing deficiently. Novels seldom spring whole and perfect from a fervid young mind. We all share Giles Gordon's dread of the moment 'when the novelist starts work, when the soaring and brilliant ideas in his head are reduced to dull words'. Getting those words to image your brilliant ideas can be like running up an endless hill with a painful heart condition.

We cannot choose our pile of sand. We can add to it, but the main substance is already there.

This is an extract from an interview with the Ghanaian writer Ama Ata Aidoo after she had visited the United States in 1967.

Aidoo: . . . the same kind of envy I entertained for Sagan as a

writer is the same type of envy I entertain for the hippie movement because it is the type of nice thing you would do if you had the chance.
Interviewer: You mean it's not really practical.
A: It comes with freedom — a certain type of freedom which I think no black person in this world has right now. It's almost like doing something which is beautiful and nice because you want to do it — like writing stories about lovers in Paris — it is beautiful, it is nice. But whereas Sagan could do it, and she does do it with a whole lot of relevance and validity, I cannot see myself as a writer writing about lovers in Accra because you see, there are so many other problems . . .
I: You feel a responsibility in fact.
A: Exactly.

The only responsibility we can have as writers is to our own pile of sand. Aidoo recognised that, and did not allow envy to warp her recognition of the relevance of what Sagan had made from her pile.

I cannot exaggerate the importance I place on her attitude.

We all experience envy — I envied Sagan when she was so successful so young — and it would be mealy-mouthed to deny it. But it must not prevent us from learning all we can from other novelists. It is one way of adding to our pile of sand, and also of helping us to define what is particular and special about it.

'What is so wonderful about great literature,' wrote Forster, 'is that it transforms the man who reads it towards the condition of the man who wrote, and brings to birth in us also the creative impulse.'

Here is John Cowper Powys on the same theme:

Perhaps the most wonderful of all thoughts, except those of love under certain very especial circumstances, are the thoughts that come to us when we have been reading some particularly thrilling book and then stop for a second to observe the shadows on the hills, or to look out upon the lights of the streets, or to gaze down at the sea.

Life provides the pile of sand. The inspiration of other writers prompts you to look for your spade and tentatively try to use it.

Unless the unpredictable forces eliminate both spade and sand, there is plenty of time to learn.

Then perhaps one day a prime minister, or a prostitute, or a poet, unable to sleep, will reach for your novel and find illumination.

You never know — it might even be read by a famous actor who will want to star in the movie. They're not all like Cary Grant.

A note to teachers regarding exercises

It is impossible to plan structured exercises for would-be novel writers; so much depends on the individual approach and needs of each student. But outlined below are tentative suggestions specifically related to some of the chapters in this book.

Beginnings

If you have an idea for a novel, try to write down any or all of the following:

What you see as the over-riding theme of the book
The opening scene
A key scene — not necessarily from near the beginning
A synopsis of the plot
A description of one of the background settings
A description of one of the main characters

For those of you who want to reach the end as soon as possible

Experiment with the narrative point of view by writing the same scene in

the first person
the third person from one viewpoint
the third person from two or more viewpoints
the third person from a general, objective viewpoint

Back to the beginning

Describe in fictional terms an activity you really enjoy
Describe in fictional terms something unpleasant that has been done to you
Describe a conventional, routine activity in fictional terms
Write personally and informally about a novel or novelist you particularly admire

Grandmothers and Paragraphs

Write a vivid description of a person;
Write a vivid description of a place;
Bring the two together in a piece of fiction.

Write, and re-write, (and re-re-write), a self-contained paragraph about anything you like until you have made it as near-perfect as possible.

Types of novel

If you are interested in a particular genre, describe what you think are its essential ingredients and cite one or two good examples.

How can I improve my novel?

If you have finished a novel, choose one of its components from the list below and try to see where you might make improvements. Perhaps talk to the class or group about this experience, giving examples of where you feel you have succeeded, and where not.

Theme and plot
Character
Dialogue
Description